Praise for Joseph Bailey and *Fearproof Your Life*

"I like this book because it provides me with physical as well as mental tools for releasing fear. It also contains fascinating methods for measuring progress. Most importantly, by guiding me in how to access my deeper Self, it ushers me into the Place where I am already free of fear. In many ways, *Fearproof Your Life* is a complete spiritual path."
—Hugh Prather, author of *Standing On My Head*

"*Fearproof Your Life* is a book for our times. Fear itself is an epidemic in our culture, and the actions that flow from fear cause much of the suffering that currently permeates our world. Joe Bailey, a powerful teacher and gifted psychotherapist, gives wise counsel on how to respond to this pervasive fear. In language that is simple and accessible, Joe guides us to find the root source of our fear—within ourselves—and then to overcome that fear, and overcome all addiction, through self-transformation. This is not an easy self-help book. It is really a book about awakening, finding freedom from fear and other attachments of the ego, and using that freedom to respond to the deep needs that we see everywhere in today's world. Inner stillness, clarity of mind, a compassionate heart, courageous action—are these not what we long for? These are the traits that Joe Bailey embodies in his own life, and shares with us all in the pages of this book. May it bring you, and this beautiful world we share, a greater sense of peace."
—Henry Emmons, MD, author of *The Chemistry of Joy: A Three-Step Program for Overcoming Depression Through Western Science and Eastern Wisdom*

"*Fearproof* is a must read for anyone who is just plain tired of living from pain, scarcity, and having a constant dull feeling. Joe knows about living from love and joy because he is joy and love! Read it and be in love!"
—Craig & Patricia Neal, Heartland, Inc.

FEARPROOF
Your Life

How to THRIVE in a
World Addicted to Fear

Joseph Bailey

Conari Press

First published in 2007 by Conari Press,
an imprint of Red Wheel/Weiser, LLC
With offices at:
500 Third Street, Suite 230
San Francisco, CA 94107
www.redwheelweiser.com

ISBN-10: 1-57324-307-8
ISBN-13: 978-1-57324-307-0

Library of Congress Cataloging-in-Publication Data

Bailey, Joseph V.
  Fearproof your life : how to thrive in a world addicted to fear / Joseph Bailey.
    p. cm.
  ISBN 1-57324-307-8 (alk. paper)
  1. Fear. I. Title.
  BF575.F2B24 2007
  152.4'6--dc22
                                        2007020515

Cover and text design by Donna Linden
Typesetting and illustrations by Landon Eber
Typeset in Gotham and Weiss
Cover photograph © Rob Casey/Brand X/Corbis

Printed in the United States of America
RRD
10 9 8 7 6 5 4 3 2 1

The paper used in this publication meets the minimum requirements of the
American National Standard for Information Sciences—Permanance of Paper for
Printed Library Materials Z39.48-1992 (R1997).

In Memory of Dr. Richard Carlson, 1961–2006
Friend, Coauthor, and Inspiration to Many

Contents

Acknowledgments

This book was inspired by the events surrounding September 11, 2001. As I witnessed people's responses to the terrorist attacks, the media's coverage, and the subsequent military and political responses, I saw the emergence of an epidemic of fear. I later realized that this obsession with fear has always been with us, but these events heightened my awareness of a world preoccupied with fear. This awareness motivated me to write a book to help in the healing of the cause of all fear—the separation from our true nature—our spiritual Self.

Since then, I have encountered many people's courageous, calming, and wise responses to this epidemic of fear. Many strangers have inspired me, whether facing a terminal illness, experiencing a catastrophe on the level of Katrina, or simply dealing with daily life in the hectic twenty-first century. I wrote this book to help me and all of us to deal with a world in the process of an enormous transformation. I want to thank all those who, simply by being themselves, have inspired me to live a fearless life.

I especially want to thank my dear friend Richard Carlson, who died shortly after writing the foreword to this book. Richard was my coauthor of *Slowing Down to the Speed of Life*. He and I were best friends and colleagues. Over the years he has encouraged all my writings but especially this book, as he saw the desire of humanity to live a fearless life. I will miss his friendship and encouragement, but I will always feel his love and influence on me as a person and as a writer.

I also want to thank my greatest supporter, teacher, and truth editor—my wife Michael. She has been my partner in the pursuit of spiritual understanding for over twenty-six years and is a constant source of joy and love. As for my friends who inspire and teach me by the lives they live, I want to thank my physical trainer, Ron Morris who has guided me to be my true Self on a physical level; my friend Karen Clark for her courageous story of cancer; my sister Ginny for her love and support and her cheerleading over the years; and to all my friends who make life worthwhile and a joy.

Professionally, I want to thank my agent, Mark Chimsky for helping me find my new publisher, Conari Press, and for always being there to encourage, challenge, and support my writing career. He is more than an agent; he is a good friend. For editorial guidance I want to thank Laurie Viera who began to polish my book at an early stage in its development. I also want to thank Caroline Pincus and her team of editors from Conari Press who took the manuscript to a new level of clarity and readability. I want to thank my publisher at Conari Press, Jan Johnson, who believed in this book from the beginning and guided in its evolution to its present form.

Foreword

Writing a quality book on the addiction to fear is no small undertaking. For a book on this subject to be truly useful to its readers, its author must embody the material and not be frightened himself. That, of course, eliminates around 99.99 percent of all authors! I was honored to be asked to write this foreword because I have had the privilege of knowing Joseph Bailey, both personally and professionally, for many, many years, and I can honestly say that he is more "at ease" with his life and less frightened than anyone I've ever known.

Being around Joe Bailey is a very comforting experience. I've personally witnessed him calm down clients, total strangers, attendees at his seminars, friends, family, and even children. It is said that everyone is at least a little frightened, but I've yet to see that with Joseph. I find that when I'm with him, my own fears begin to disappear. His message is powerful and contagious. It's also extremely easy to understand. No psychobabble here. Just excellent, heartfelt information that really solves the problem. After reading this book, my sense is that you, too, will feel his comfort.

By the way, if you ever have a chance to see Joseph speak at a seminar or book signing, I encourage you to make the effort. It could change your life. Joseph is a fearless speaker, and in my opinion one of the best and most profound speakers in the world.

Fear has become rampant in our own culture. It dominates our minds as well as our media. Fear is responsible for all hatred, wars, greed, and other subhuman qualities. It is also used as a tool of manipulation by those wishing to keep us frightened as a means of staying in power. We have no shortage of reasons to eliminate fear in our world.

Fearproof Your Life is a book on how to have a permanent change of heart regarding fear. You will learn so much about fear in this book—where it originates (not where you might imagine), what keeps it going, and, most important, how to let it go. I encourage you to pay particular attention to two things: where fear comes from—no exceptions—and how to eliminate it from your life forever.

In the absence of fear, your life will never be the same. You'll be more confident, of course, but you'll also be free to experience tremendous intimacy with others and take appropriate risks, all without fear. Life with less fear is not only more rewarding and nourishing, but it's a lot more fun too!

In this book, you'll learn the invaluable tool of reflection, and how reflection can add depth and security to your life. Since fear is such an overwhelming problem in our culture, there could not be a more important book in my eyes. I believe this book should be required reading in schools. If it were, we'd live in a much less frightened world. I'll be giving this book to almost everyone I know!

I read this book in just two delicious sittings, meaning I could not put it down. Having been someone who has been frightened on many occasions, I feel very grateful that Joseph Bailey has written this book. I'm certain that my fear will never dominate my life again, and I'm confident that you will join me after enjoying this tremendous book, which I highly and enthusiastically recommend.

Richard Carlson,
somewhere on the coast of Northern California, fall 2006

CHAPTER 1
A World Addicted to Fear

The Epidemic of Fear

If you find yourself awakening in the middle of the night with worries about the previous day or the next day, you are not alone. *How will that meeting go tomorrow? Will my boss like my ideas? Will that woman I like be as attracted to me as I am to her? I hope my kids are okay! When will the terrorists strike again? Is my 401(k) secure? Will there be enough left at retirement the way the economy is going now? What is that pain in my stomach; am I getting cancer? Will I pass my test tomorrow?* These worries are all common expressions of the same emotion—fear.

Our wonderings, worries, analyzing, projections, and obsessions have become the relentless drone of our thinking for many of us today. But is this really a recent habit, or have we always been addicted to our worrisome thoughts? Have they only just recently grown to epidemic proportions of stress, anxiety, and dread about the future?

As a psychologist and addictions counselor for the past thirty years, I have witnessed one underlying constant in the litany of addictions and mental disorders in my patients, and in the worries and anxiety of my colleagues and myself—*fear.* The specific thing each of us fears and the level of intensity of that fear varies from person to person and from time to time. Nevertheless, fear is the constant, whatever its form or intensity.

Fear is so commonplace that it seems necessary, normal, and in some cases a sign of true caring, awareness, responsibility, and maturity. For example, our society sees worrying about our kids as a sign of being a loving parent. Fear is such an accepted part of life that we even brag about our fears: Who is most stressed? Who has more to worry about? What's fascinating is that we don't think of stress or worry as fear, but that is all it is—fear in a socially acceptable form. Fear appears *normal*, but is it just so commonplace that it only *seems* normal? Is it simply part of our collective (un)consciousness? I believe it is.

Aside from our everyday personal fears concerning safety, having enough, being successful, child rearing, performance, finances, and relationships, we also worry about the "big stuff." The news is full of daily reports of ever-more-violent deaths from terrorism. Government intelligence sources promise that attacks by the invisible enemy on our sovereign soil could happen anywhere, anytime. The future of the economy seems more uncertain, with the national debt at record levels, our currency devalued, and rampant corruption in our corporations and financial institutions. The environment is also cause for fear—global warming, climatic catastrophes, deforestation, extinction of animals and plant life, and pollution of our air, water, and soil. Who wouldn't be afraid? There doesn't appear to be a choice.

Is fear the logical response? If so, shouldn't it motivate us to do something about all the problems? One would think so, but the opposite is often the case. Fear has gotten so intense that we often feel almost immobilized by it, even numbed. This numbness is a defense against our feeling overwhelmed by the number and magnitude of personal and societal problems.

The other day I was visiting my ninety-eight-year-old friend in her nursing home. Though she was very glad to see me, she didn't even turn off the TV when I came into her room. She could not risk missing the latest on the terrorist situation, which is why she is glued to the cable news station all her waking hours. She feels she cannot risk being caught off guard.

My friend had always been an example of courage, whether it was climbing mountains in Glacier Park or fighting for a political issue. She had been an inspiration to me all my life. I have seen my friend transform from a vibrant, alive, aware person to one who is trapped by her fearful thoughts.

The illusion that safety comes from being informed of each detail has many of us addicted to cable news. It is like a scary mystery novel that we can't put down till we see how it ends. Unfortunately, in real life the story never ends, so we never get to put the novel down. Following the news, reading the never-ending novel, *becomes* our life.

It is no accident that following the news has become our life. Advertisers, the media, movie producers, and politicians know that fear captivates an audience and motivates them to stay tuned, buy the product, vote for the politician who is pushing the greatest fears, and join the group that promises the most protection. Fear is addicting, and the policymakers of all organizations know it. The pushers of fear are selling a product, and we have bought it wholesale.

Addicted to Fear

Worry, anxiety, dread, obsession, where do they come from? Throughout time, humankind has sought peace and safety by trying to outguess the unknown. We have tried to anticipate and prepare for the unexpected, the imagined, the apparitions of our minds. Our efforts to control the unknown and thus keep ourselves safe have led to a collective as well as a personal sensation of fear. Individually and as a society, we have become addicted to fear.

Instead of preparing us for an unknown future, fear locks us in an illusionary sand castle of protection, a false sense of security from demons, dangers, and all that we dread. Each day the tide of reality and truth sweeps in and destroys our tentative hold on security, and the sand castle washes back into the sea of creation. Yet no matter how often the sand castle of illusory control is destroyed, the ego rebuilds it with fearful, vigilant thoughts that keep us from experiencing true peace of mind and the ultimate comfort of truth.

This cycle of fear has all the trappings and symptoms of any addiction: denial, rationalization, projection, increased tolerance to the substance (in this case, fear), imbalance that seems normal, and increased harmful and fatal consequences that we minimize and blame on others. We have come to grips with many of humanity's addictions and brought them out of the closet of denial. Alcoholism, drug addiction, compulsive gambling, and sex addiction are the most common. Fear, however, is the last bastion of our collective denial of a self-destructive disease. *Furthermore, fear is at the very core of all the other addictions and negativity in our world.*

Fear is the cause of all war, greed, material and spiritual poverty, destruction of the planet, and inhumanity to ourselves and to one another. Fear manifests in less noticeable, less dramatic ways as well. For fear is the most insidious force in our world today, robbing all of us—not just those whose fears have warranted a diagnosis of mental illness or a label of addiction—of our capacity for peace of mind, bodily and spiritual well-being, and an ability to get along with each other in a life-sustaining and harmonious manner.

My Addiction to Fear

I remember the first time I felt the beginnings of my addiction to fear. I was five years old, and kindergarten was about to begin. Up to that point in time I had lived a carefree, happy-go-lucky life. The thought of leaving my family, my home, and all that was familiar to me and venturing off on a bus to a strange and unknown place terrified me; so much so that my mom decided to hold me back from going to school till first grade.

Thus began my intimate relationship with fear for the next thirty-some-odd years. In grade school I developed a school phobia and would become so anxious in the morning that I got sick to my stomach before school each day. In high school my fear addiction grew—test anxiety, dating, college admissions tests, peer pressure, career choices. I got to the point where my day began with a pit in my stomach, and I would immediately begin thinking up a list of worries before I got out of bed. I was addicted to fear, but I didn't know it. In my home, worry was simply a normal part of life.

In college, my level of fear grew to the point that I actually had a few panic attacks around exam time. I had no idea that it was unnatural for me to feel so fearful, and I had no idea how to stop the fear. I just coped with it by trying to work harder and achieve higher grades in school and to understand it intellectually by studying psychology. I also occasionally blew off steam by drinking alcohol, which gave me some momentary relief. It got to the point that if I didn't feel fear, I would wonder what I was avoiding and immediately begin searching for something to be afraid of. I was like a swiveling radar dish, always on the alert for something to fear, to avoid, or to be on the lookout for.

I see clearly now why I went into the field of psychology. I instinctively knew that fear was unhealthy, but I had no hope or understanding of how to let it go. In fact, a part of me didn't want to let it go. I was hooked! Nevertheless, I read books on meditation, took yoga classes, did stress-relieving breathing practices, and began to search for peace of mind in whatever way I could attain it. I engaged in many techniques to cope with stress and even taught many seminars on stress reduction. But I was still afraid.

Then, twenty-five years ago, I discovered the connection between my power to think and my experience of anxiety. I realized that fear comes from within my own state of mind and does not originate in the unknown, outside circumstances or events.

Once I realized the origin of my fears, my stress went away, almost immediately. Once I quit believing everything I thought and realized I was the thinker and creator of those thoughts, I began to identify with my deeper intelligence—my true Self. My life of headaches, insomnia, back pain, and nervous stomach were gone.

Today I have very little fear. I am no longer afraid of fear, nor do I take it as truth. Instead, I see it as nothing more than a friendly guidance system, which is a concept I explore later in this book. I am writing this book because of my own realization of how to live a fearless life and the desire to share that understanding with you. Fear keeps us in that sand castle of illusionary safety, but it doesn't ever really protect us. In fact, fear is our undoing. This book will help you realize this truth and show you how to discover a source of security, knowing, and serenity that lies within you, and within each of us—the true Self.

From Coping to a Change of Heart

How do we cope with our fear? Some of us nostalgically try to turn the clock back to a time when we believe that values were more wholesome and life was simpler and more secure. (We tend to forget that those simpler times had their own set of fears, such as the bomb shelters and nuclear threat of the 1950s.) Some of us push headlong into denial and self-destructive distractions via addictions to drugs, alcohol, food, sex, money, or gambling. Many of us look outside to saviors—radio pundits, TV preachers, religious or psychological authority figures—in an effort to find someone who has the answers to life's current anxiety, emptiness, and uncertainty. We turn outside and look to Oprah, Dr. Phil, and a host of others, hoping they will give us the coping mechanisms we need to live in an age of anxiety.

Figure 1 illustrates some of the ways in which we have coped with this all-pervasive fear.

Coping mechanisms allow us to live with our dysfunctions without really changing. They are like solving the problem of drowning in a leaky canoe by constantly having to bail out the water instead of patching up the leaks.

For example, if I am afraid and feel anxious, I may have a drink to alleviate my anxiety. My anxiety may go away momentarily, but when I sober up the anxiety is back (with a hangover), and nothing has really changed *internally*.

The same is true with a positive coping mechanism like jogging or journaling, but without the hangover. With positive coping mechanisms as well as negative ones, we are able to cope with a faulty perception of reality, one that is not based on our true Self, our spiritual nature. That faulty perception is a projection of our ego thought system—our interpretations, prejudices, and biases.

In contrast, a "change of heart" would be a shift in our level of consciousness. It is looking at what I am afraid of from the perspective of the true Self rather than my ego's limited thought

Figure 1 COPING WITH FEAR

system. It is an internal change that transforms the pattern of my thoughts, and as a result my attitude changes as well.

Fearproof Your Life is about how to realize that shift in consciousness, that change of heart. It is about empowering ourselves to realize that *we are the creators of our experience*. It is about reminding ourselves that we are the ones who created the fear, and thus we are the ones who can uncreate it.

If you have already chosen this path or are willing to pursue it, even if you aren't certain it can happen for you, then this book is for you. If you want a life that is fearless, a life of certainty of the truth, a life of love, joy, and peace, this book can help guide you there.

Somehow, deep inside, you know that *within you is the secret to living a whole and fearless life*. How do you know this? Because inside you, inside everyone, there is a Universal Intelligence that has guided you to this point.

This book will show you how to access this Universal Intelligence. It will show you that your true nature is trustworthy, and it will show you how to choose it as a source of reliable wisdom. This path goes beyond a life of coping mechanisms designed to deal with fear; instead it promises a life without fear— a life that is fearproof.

As with any addiction, we can only continue the addiction as long as we are in denial and under the delusion that there is no problem. *Fearproof Your Life* is a book that attempts to break us out of our delusion and begin the process of recovery from our individual and collective addiction to fear. Instead of managing our addiction to fear by developing coping mechanisms, other addictions, and belief systems that we rigidly cling to, we can discover something that is more lasting, more truthful, and more effective. We can alleviate and conquer our fear by discovering *who we are*.

CHAPTER 2
Fear: Friend or Foe?

We are both drawn to and repelled by fear. Though we often complain of stress, anxiety, and overwhelming fear of the unknown, we seem drawn to fear like a moth to a flame. We love frightening movies, adrenaline-rush sports, reality TV shows such as *Fear Factor*, and scary bedtime stories. And although we may not like the frightening news on TV, fear is what motivates us to stay tuned. News producers are well aware of this fact, which is why they usually lead with a fear-invoking story.

Despite our attraction to fear, we don't want it to strike too close to home because we hate the way it makes us feel. Fear makes our palms sweat, our hearts race, our breathing strain, and our muscles tense, which over time can lead to physical and mental illnesses. Sustained fear leads to stress, anxiety, phobias, insomnia, and panic attacks.

On a societal level, fear has become an epidemic. We live in constant fear of the unknown—terrorism, crime, the weather, the uncertainty of our health, the economy, and the future of our country and planet.

On a personal level, worry, stress, dread, and concern are considered normal, even desirable. We worry about our children's safety and their future. We worry about the security of our finances, investments, retirement, insurance, and having "enough." We fear for our physical and mental well-being, while commercials for prescriptions to treat every imaginable ailment feed that fear. We are concerned about relationships—finding one, keeping one, getting out of one. Despite our attraction to fear, it inhibits our actions, limits our choices, and keeps our world small. It keeps us from taking risks, from following our dreams, from telling the truth, from expressing ourselves honestly, from feeling hope for the future, and from doing what we want to do *freely.*

We seem to need fear, but clearly it can be a destructive force in our lives. Could it be that this all-encompassing emotion has a purpose?

The Distortion of Fear

Fear becomes contaminated and distorted when we lose faith in its overall protective nature, when we feel separate from the Divine whole. Instead of listening to and trusting fear's alert system to be there when we need it, the ego takes over and uses the intellect to project into the world all the possible things that *could* go wrong. We quit trusting in the information that will come to us when we need it and thus begin to trust in the false, ego-based system of fear.

Ego-based fear is distorted and contaminated. With the help of the intellect, it projects dangers that aren't there, only imagined. In its most extreme distortion, ego-based fear has resulted in obsessive-compulsive personalities like that of Howard Hughes, the brilliant entrepreneur who became such a prisoner of his fears of germs and enemies that for the later part of his life he sequestered himself in a tomblike existence in his Las Vegas penthouse. Though he was one of the richest men on Earth, Hughes lived an emotionally impoverished existence.

On a more ordinary level, ongoing ego-based fear creates chronic emotional and chemical imbalances, which in turn can lead to physical and emotional discomfort and disease.

Fear as a tool of the ego:

- Imagines danger that doesn't exist
- Keeps the body in a state of constant imbalance

- Leads to chemical imbalances that cause illness and unhealthy behavior
- Causes disproportionate reactions (road rage, violence, panic attacks) to normal situations, and
- Robs us of our enjoyment of the moment and of everyday life.

Remember that the emotion of fear can be rooted in the true Self or in the ego self. When it is rooted in the true Self, fear is acting in the service of our survival and well-being. It is a signal from the Universal Intelligence to help guide us toward safety, harmony, and a peaceful life. When the emotion of fear stems from the ego, it is self-destructive and creates disharmony within our bodies and our emotions, and between our fellow human beings and ourselves.

Figure 2 THE CYCLE OF FEAR ADDICTION

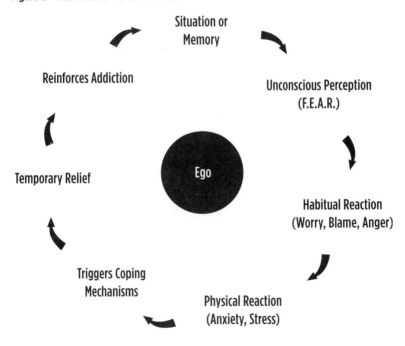

The Wisdom of Fear

Fear has the same purpose as physical pain. Pain is a necessary sensation that lets us know when we feel sick or well, comfortable or uncomfortable, hot or cold. It is information that allows us to regulate our behavior, our temperature, our food intake, amount of exercise, level of activity and sleep, and a host of other factors that can lead to either equilibrium or imbalance.

The true purpose of fear is meant to be a signal that alerts us to danger and the need to take appropriate action. As a Divine tool, that signal can be in the form of a racing heart, shortness of breath, or sweaty palms, which are only a few of the sensations that we associate with fear. When we feel fear, our body responds through the adrenals and kidneys to give us a burst of energy to deal with the situation, known as the fight-or-flight response. In this way fear is a very useful emotion for our survival and well-being.

When properly understood, fear is like a psychic radar system that alerts us to present dangers, such as an oncoming car in our lane, a tornado alert, or a criminal perpetrator in our midst. Fear can also remind us to prepare for future needs, such as saving for retirement, fixing a leaky roof, or maintaining our cars.

Fear as a Divine tool:

- Warns us of danger
- Energizes our bodies and minds to respond appropriately and intelligently to situations, and
- Serves as an intuitive radar system for unknown dangers, such as earthquakes, storms, or attacks.

As a Divine tool, fear has another purpose: to let us know when we are moving away from the wisdom and safety of our true Selves and into the imbalance of the separated state of the ego. Fear tells us that we have let our ego self pull us into a world of habitual dread, a never-ending chain of projection, reaction, and self-fulfilling prophecy. In particular, fear informs us when we are getting caught up in unhealthy thoughts about the future. When we try to figure out or predict the unknown with our intellect, we feel fearful. *What if this happens? What if that happens?* The "what ifs" coupled with obsessive thinking are what cause the imbalance of fear.

We may not like how fear feels, but when we see its true purpose we realize that the sensation of fear is as necessary to our emotional and spiritual well-being as physical pain is to the survival and health of the body. All we have to do is recognize our fear as a friend who is trying to warn us that we have veered off track. The key to transforming fear into information and healing is to accept it instead of judge it and return to the emotional stability of our true Selves, which will always guide us and provide us with the wisdom we need to take appropriate action and stay safe.

How do we discern the difference between the healthy and unhealthy sources of fear?

Fear as a Guidance System

Let's explore the process of how we can interpret or misinterpret fear when it shows up. The sensations we interpret as fear are a guidance system, divinely designed to keep us on the straight and narrow path of balance, health, and happiness. They are like the lane grooves on the side of the highway that warn us that we are wandering off the main road, onto the shoulder, and ultimately into the ditch of our habitual, ego-based thinking. Fear itself doesn't damage our psyche any more than speed bumps damage our car. It is only when we ignore or misinterpret the information of the bumps that we enter the uncomfortable state of fear that we are so familiar with. When we listen to these same sensations from our true Selves, we receive wise information and insights that guide our lives.

Sensation Viewed from True Self

Sensation → Viewed as natural information → Insight →
Action that leads to balance and health → Harmony with others

---

Recognizing and Responding to the Sensations of Fear

How do we know that we are in a state of fear imbalance and need to return to our true Selves? Fear speaks to us, as do all feelings, in the form of a *sensation*. Sensations of fear imbalance include tightness of muscles (neck, back, shoulders, jaw, and stomach are the most common), shortness or irregularity of breath, increased heart rate, extremes of body temperature (shivering or sweating), indigestion (nausea, diarrhea, vomiting), irregularities of movement (jumpiness, fidgeting, facial twitches, furrowed brow, clumsiness, lack of coordination), and disruptive thinking patterns (confusion, forgetfulness, distraction, busy mind, irritability, obsessiveness, defensiveness, paranoia, and a host of other conditions).

These sensations are there not to be analyzed but rather to remind us to calm down, listen, and reflect in the moment. If we ignore them, they become even more intense in order to gain our attention. Denial of these sensations is just as dangerous as obsessing over them. Overconfidence and arrogance will be the result, and we may end up in the ditch.

When we finally do calm down and listen, we hear the wisdom of our true Selves speaking to us about what action to take, what thought to ignore, what adaptation to make. The voice of our true Selves is there to guide us back to sanity, peace of mind, and clarity of thinking. It is there to give us insights that make our lives travel smoothly down the road of our Divine destiny.

When we don't know how to become quiet and listen to that voice, we depend on our intellect to try and figure out what is going to happen and how best to prepare for it. Information from the intellect is limited to what we already know, to our memories and beliefs. If we limit ourselves to this base of knowledge, we can't help but worry and obsess about the "what ifs"—which blind us from seeing possible new options.

Sensation Viewed from Ego Self

Sensation → Projection/Interpretation from ego → Fear →
Reaction that leads to imbalance and disease → Division, violence, war

When we react from the ego self, we get into our heads and start analyzing, remembering, comparing, and then projecting our interpretations and future worries onto the situation we are currently experiencing. Doing this amps up the fear, anxiety, stress, and worry, which throw us off balance physically and emotionally. As a result, our thinking becomes confused, prejudiced, and sometimes even irrational.

Transforming Fear to Calm

Figure 3 is a diagram of how we have the choice and power to transform fear, any fear, to calm. Even in the face of danger or misfortune, we are capable of living from a state of calm. It depends totally on where we place our attention and consciousness.

Figure 3   TRANSFORMING FEAR TO CALM

Sensation of fear → Acceptance of fear, staying calm →
See possible choices that are positive and nonlimiting →
Positive and empowered action →
Neutralized effect of outside events and other people →
Increased freedom and well-being

When we accept our fear yet see that it has no power over us, we see that *we have a choice*—a choice to be affected or not. Fear is not there to do anything but get our attention, raise our awareness. From the standpoint of our true Self, we are able to discern what to do with the information that is coming through the sensations. We *know* if we are to act on the information and avoid the danger, make a healthy choice, or disregard the sensation because we realize it is coming from a "phantom fear," that is, a past conditioned reaction that has no true relevance to our current situation. From a state of calm observation, without judging our fear or becoming afraid of the fear itself, we gain a perspective known as *discernment.*

For example, the other day I was taking an exercise class. At one particularly strenuous part of the workout I began to experience numbness in my head, lightheadedness, and shortness of breath. I began to feel fear. My head raced with thoughts of a stroke or heart attack, since my best friend had just had a heart attack and bypass surgery two weeks previously. I scared myself with those thoughts, which exacerbated the hyperventilation and my other symptoms.

I paused in my workout and took a moment to regain my breath and my calm. I asked my trainer about what was happening, and he asked if I was holding my breath and keeping my neck tight. Upon reflection I realized that indeed I was keeping my neck tight and restricting my breath to my upper chest rather than taking deep, lower abdominal breaths. He then told me that there is a nerve in the neck that when pinched (from the tightness of my posture) will cause those exact symptoms.

As I continued the workout I became conscious of holding my neck tight and would then release it consciously. My numbness, lightheadedness, and dizziness subsided. What could have been a Woody Allen–style bout of hypochondria, ending with visions of a brain tumor and death, transformed into a helpful insight about my workout. Taking a moment to reflect and asking for information from a trained professional resulted in a positive outcome and the capacity to see the situation from my wise true Self.

If I had begun to project from my ego state during my exercise class, I may have stopped working out altogether. I could have thought, *I'm getting too old for this. I might be risking my life doing these silly exercise classes! How could the instructor have me do something as dangerous as that? How could he be so stupid?*

Understanding and realizing when our ego takes charge can prevent us from making decisions that limit our health, our activities, and our choices. Knowing that we have a choice—to rely on our fear-based ego or our wise true Self—is true freedom and liberation. Now we have the wisdom and the knowledge to break this vicious cycle of fear both personally and as a planet, *if* we are willing.

Fear of Flying

Two friends of mine recently took a trip, illustrating the contrast between taking your fearful thoughts seriously or not. Jeanie was traveling with her sister Sara on vacation. Sara is very fearful about travel and Jeanie is not. All Sara could think about as the trip approached was everything that could go wrong—on the flight, with customs, with baggage, and their hotel accommodations—

plus a host of other worries. Jeanie tried to reassure her sister, but Sara's mind was set. This is what a *mindset* is.

The day of travel finally arrived, and in her anxiety about all the details of the trip, Sara forgot to bring her passport and they had to change to a later flight. Immediately, Sara got angry with all the terrorists for the tightened security and the hassles that are now a normal part of airline travel. By the time she did arrive at their travel destination, the die was cast. She could tell she was going to have a miserable time. By not recognizing her fear as a signal that she was off track, she spiraled into a series of projections and reactions at every step of her journey. As a result, she didn't have much of a good time and wasn't a particularly pleasant travel partner for Jeanie. Sara had innocently and unconsciously chosen her mindset of fear, and thus she viewed her entire situation through this lens.

As for Jeanie, she had a great time despite Sara's gloom-and-doom mood. She could see that Sara was, as always, making everything a big deal. But she also knew her sister well enough to understand why she reacted as she did, and it became part of the trip's entertainment to her. Nothing was going to ruin Jeanie's vacation because she knew where her experience was coming from—*her own thinking*. Of course there were hiccups along the way, as any trip has, but she took them in stride instead of taking them personally. As a result she had a great vacation. Eventually, even Sara lightened up and relaxed more as the vacation went on. Jeanie's joyful serenity couldn't help but rub off on Sara, despite Sara's best efforts to resist it.

Was Sara so wrong to be afraid? With all that is going on in the world, aren't her fears somewhat justified? And don't our fears lead us to take necessary precautions against possible dangers or worst-case scenarios, such as having survival equipment in our car or boat or improving airport and harbor security?

Yes, it is true that the sensation we associate with fear can alert us to do something to prepare for a future event. But there is a difference between preparing and obsessing, or between having an insight and projecting. Fear, if unchecked, can block clear thinking, reason, instinct, and creativity. It can take us into the illusionary safety and familiarity of our belief systems, which are based only on our past experiences and preconceived perceptions. Sara's preoccupation with her fears kept her mind so busy and distracted that not only was she *unable* to enjoy the sights and activities of her trip, but she actually made herself more vulnerable to potential dangers like pickpockets because she was less aware of her surroundings.

If our fear is unconscious, it can cause us to jump to prejudiced conclusions, and thus we can blame the wrong person or cause for a present difficulty or even a crime. In Sara's case, she blamed the frightening state of the world for her failure to remember her passport. Ego-based fear lowers the veil of our belief systems, positive or negative, over our perception of the here and now, thus obscuring the truth of *what is* or what actually did happen. And if we operate with obscured vision, we can put ourselves in danger.

In Sara's case, all her past bad experiences of vacations and travel came flooding in, and she took them all as ironclad truth to be applied to the here and now, rather than just her thinking about past events, which could only have power in the present if she allowed it to do so. Jeanie had some of the same thoughts pass through her mind, but she chose to focus her attention on having a good time instead of analyzing what could go wrong. By trusting in her true Self to alert her to any danger through intuition, she was able to free herself to enjoy her journey. When we are calm and in a balanced state of mind, we have 360 degrees of awareness, rather than the tunnel vision of fear, which blinds us to life's potential dangers and pitfalls.

The phrase "blinded by fear" refers to these phenomena. Fear limits us perceptually to see only that which we fear rather than opportunities, insights, and other dangers we haven't considered. On the other hand, a feeling of calm awareness doesn't limit the scope of our perception. Like an athlete in "the zone," calm awareness is broad focus that allows us to prepare for the unexpected. If people really took this one point to heart, their lives would change from frenzied vigilance to serene awareness.

Our Internal Alarm Clock

Another helpful way to think about fear is as an alarm clock. When we hear the alarm clock of fear, it is there to get our attention, to wake us up to the need to become *more conscious*. But once we are awake we don't let our alarm clock keep ringing. The ringing would be annoying and unnecessary and would disrupt the tranquility of our day, just as sustained fear disrupts the tranquility of our minds.

It is only upon reflection that we learn what set off the alarm: either our faulty thinking or a need to take remedial action. The alarm clock of fear may be trying to wake us up to the fact that our own thoughts are terrorizing us. It may be trying to tell us that these thoughts are only a remnant of the past and have nothing to do with our present circumstances, and that we need to let go of them. Conversely, fear may be waking us up to our need to reflect or act on a problem with our job, or a parenting issue, or a financial decision, or the threat of imminent danger.

When we view our fearful thoughts from a fully awake, conscious mind, we have the wise power of *discernment* on our side. When we are conscious and aware, we can also see if there is anything we need to do to change or prepare for a situation. But if we keep the alarm of fear ringing while we are attempting to discern what to change or do, the ringing of fear in our heads will become a distraction and cause more fear. That is why it is best to listen to fear only long enough to wake up, and then remember that behind it is information as to what, if anything, to change or do.

Blinded by Fear

Many years ago, I taught people about the power of fear through rock climbing. My colleague and I would take people climbing to help them learn about themselves and how to work with and trust others. Initially, the fear of falling down the cliff would often paralyze people emotionally or keep them stuck on one part of the climb for a very long time. To them, the rock looked impossible to climb, though it was actually quite easy and safe. The fear of falling and possibly dying kept them from seeing the easy route up the mountain. It also kept them from enjoying the experience.

From time to time, my colleague and I would do an experiment and blindfold the participants during a climb. This was not a cruel hoax, but an opportunity to demonstrate how *fear blinds us to opportunity*. (The participants were, of course, safely tied in with a rope.) We would instruct them to feel the rock to find a handhold or foothold, completely dependent on the sense of touch. They were amazed at how easy it was to find a hold in the same place on the rock that had looked impossible to them a moment before when they had the use of their vision. They had been blinded by their fearful thoughts of what might happen, distracted by the constant ringing of the fear alarm in their heads. The initial sensation of fear, however, was meant to alert them to the necessity of thinking through the details of proper knot tying and other safety issues in order to protect themselves, but not to obsess on the danger.

When we don't understand that fear is our wake-up call to become more conscious, we can become immobilized by it. Instead of taking in information that is crucial for our safety and well-being, our unchecked fear blinds us to opportunities for dealing effectively with danger and the unknown. Unconscious fear keeps us trapped in our belief systems and past experiences, thus limiting our ability to think creatively and boundlessly in the moment. In our current world of terror, in which we worry about not only violent attacks, but about issues such as global warming and mass starvation, it behooves us to act not from fear and panic but from wisdom and clear, calm resolve.

When we recognize that being in a state of fear means that we are caught in our own ego thoughts, we are able to let go of the thinking that is creating the fear. It is then that the obvious possibilities before us reveal themselves. From a calm and clear state of mind, we are able to solve problems, respond to real danger in an intelligent and responsive manner, avoid hurting others or ourselves, and increase our chances for survival and a healthy, successful life.

When the Twin Towers of the World Trade Center were hit on September 11, 2001, many people in the buildings rushed to the elevators to escape the horror that was happening around them. One such elevator was halfway down when it malfunctioned and was stuck between floors. The elevator was filled with highly educated executives who were terrified and panicked, and one window washer named Juan Cortero. At first, several people started screaming for help, but no one heard them amidst the roar of the fire sirens and mayhem. In a calm voice Juan suggested they use his equipment to try to pry the doors open. Some people kept screaming, but Juan's calm resolve and leadership eventually led to teamwork and perseverance by the group. In the end, they were able to jimmy the doors open, and they were all saved.

Juan didn't panic or become overwhelmed by his fear, though I imagine he must have experienced the same sensations as the others. After all, he was in the same dangerous situation as the others. Nevertheless, his calm wisdom led to an insight that saved their lives. This is a powerful example of how a calm mind, regardless of its level of formal education, can bring more intelligence to a situation than a busy mind with all of its finely honed management skills.

The Rabbit's Foot of Fear: A False Sense of Protection

Juan Cortero's story demonstrates, without a doubt, the benefit of transforming fear into calm so that our inner wisdom can guide us to safety. Yet even after hearing a story like that, many people still feel a tremendous resistance to giving up their dependency on fear. A parent friend of mine put it this way: "I think we have a superstition about fear and worry. We believe that if we anticipate the worst possible scenario, then we can somehow control it. If I can imagine the worst, then it won't happen. We live in an illusion of control over our children's welfare. As a mom I would worry constantly about my kids, and when the thing I had worried about didn't happen, I would say, 'See, it worked!' Then, if something else happened, I would think, 'I should have worried about that.'"

For my friend, as for many of us, the act of worrying has become a superstitious habit to ward off danger. Over time, it becomes more than a habit; it becomes an addiction. This addiction to fear is the most basic form of superstition: *If I worry enough, it won't happen. And if it does, I'll be prepared and not caught off guard.* Thus we have acquired what amounts to a rabbit's foot of fear to ward off future danger and protect us from the unknown.

We erroneously believe that we can maintain a mindset toward life that is fear-based and still feel comfortable. We long to feel relief from the discomfort of fear, but we don't want to give it up. We're afraid that if we do, we will let down our guard and lose our protection against all the danger "out there." We actually believe that living in fear is a worthwhile caution that keeps us safe. We fool ourselves into believing that by identifying all potential dangers and keeping our worlds small, we can control and predict all unknown variables. In our arrogance to presume we can know all dangers, we become prisoners of our own thinking. The end result of indulging in this habit is becoming *addicted* to fear. An addiction is anything we do that is harmful to us that we can't stop doing.

When we adopt this rationale of thinking, our lives become ruled by fear, robbing us of peace of mind and making us overly protective parents. Somehow we have associated feeling love for our children with worrying about everything that could go wrong in their lives. Our worries send them a message that the world is an unsafe place and that they are unsafe. Our worries sentence them to a life of fear, for they will use us as role models.

However, if we see fear for what its true purpose is—to wake us up to the need to listen within—then we can use fear as a guidance system to get ourselves back on track, not only for our sake, but for the sake of our children.

The daughter of a friend of ours was raised on this wisdom. Whenever Susie's parents would have a concern about her, they saw their concern as a sign that they needed to listen and reflect about that particular area of their daughter's life rather than let their concern turn to fearful thoughts about her. They were even able to take this approach in dealing with Susie's curiosity about drugs and alcohol.

On one such occasion, Susie felt particularly pressured by her boyfriend to try pot. Her parents, Tom and Jean, were of course worried about what Susie would do. Instead of reacting from fear, however, they calmed down and talked to each other about it. They decided that when the appropriate moment arrived they would talk to Susie about what they felt and would listen to her—not from a place of fear, but from a place of wise reflection. They ended up having a very open and illuminating talk about chemical use, and though Susie did engage in some minor experimentation, she never abused drugs or alcohol like many of her friends. She later realized that her boyfriend had a problem with drugs and decided to end the relationship.

The result of this type of parenting is a daughter who lives her life from joy rather than fear, and who sees life as made up of unlimited possibilities. Living fearlessly has led Susie to a high level of success, academically and athletically. Most important, she lives from a base of security and confidence in herself and in her common sense. She loves life and is not afraid of the future. She listens to herself and trusts what she hears.

To me, this is what parenting is about—teaching our children to listen to and trust themselves. When we empower our children in this way, they are not immobilized by the thoughts of the unknown future. On the contrary, they feel prepared to embrace its unlimited potential.

Breaking Our Addiction to Fear

Fear can and has become an addiction, not only to many individuals but to our society as a whole. We can become addicted to watching the news shows, to finding the most advanced security system for our homes, to obsessing about our health and the fear of death, to limiting our travel, our lifestyle, and our relationships—all because of *fear.* An addiction is anything that becomes all consuming in our lives, a preoccupation that we have an inability to live without it.

Instead of facing our addiction head-on in ourselves and in our society, we have turned to *managing* our addiction. An alcoholic will often try to manage their drinking by creating limits like "never before five o'clock" or "I only drink beer, not hard stuff." These rationalizations never work, but serve to take the addict further into their delusion of control.

In the same way, we as a society and as individuals think that if we spend enough money on defense and homeland security, better dead bolt systems and alarms to protect our homes, or if we find and destroy all the terrorists in the world, we will have less fear. In point of fact, the more we obsess about how to eliminate the grip of fear on our lives, the more fear controls us. Until we face the real cause of fear—*our thinking and the unhealthy way we use it*—we will have *zero* control over fear. Only by recognizing the true purpose of fear—*to guide us back to the wisdom of calm and our true Selves*—will we regain our freedom from fear and break our addiction to it.

As Franklin D. Roosevelt said, "We have nothing to fear but fear itself." When we become addicted to fear, our lives become consumed with it and we perpetuate an atmosphere of fear in our world.

The Possibility of a Fearless Life

Are you open to the possibility that you can discover how to live a life without fear? What if it is possible? What do you have to lose in venturing down this path?

For this moment, could you put aside what you think you know about fear and be *willing* to consider the possibility that you could live a life without fear?

The Protection of Calm

When we live our own lives from the calm, fearless knowing of our true Selves, we are able to make choices that *feel right*. They feel right because they *are right*—they are in alignment with that part of all us that is *one* with everyone.

Don't just take my word for it. Experiment with not acting from fear. Instead, use fear as a signal to calm down and reflect, and see what happens. See if you get insights about whatever is your current issue. If you do, act on those insights and see what happens. Does it feel right? How did it work out? Let your own life instruct you about your capacity for wisdom.

You can look within and consciously choose to see your Divine point of view. Making choices from your true Self is the secret to living a fearless life. It is also the secret to living a happy and successful life.

In the next chapter we explore the power of choice in creating a fearless life.

REMINDERS

1. Living from a state of fear imbalance blocks creativity, enjoyment, freedom of choice, and happiness.
2. Misinterpreted fear is the result of living in a state of separation from our true Selves.
3. Unchecked fear and worry are addictive because they give us the illusion of control over the unknown.
4. Fear is a friendly guidance system.
5. Fear is sensory information that helps us be aware of the need to return to our conscious and aware Self.
6. Fear is an alarm clock reminding us to wake up and listen to the wisdom of our true Self.

CHAPTER 3
Overcoming Fear Through Transformation
FROM EGO TO TRUE SELF

There is an old Native American story about three gods who are arguing about where to hide truth from mankind.

The first god says, "Let us hide it on the top of the highest mountain peak in the world. It is very steep and difficult to get to, extremely cold, and has almost no oxygen. Surely no one would want to go there."

The second god does not agree. "These human beings are very curious. Sooner or later they will want to see what it is like to climb that mountain, and they will find the truth. It would be far better to hide truth at the bottom of the deepest ocean where no life can survive and no man can swim that deep. They will never find it there."

The third god sits quietly and in deep reflection. Finally they turn to him and ask him where he would hide truth.

He says, "I agree that both of these are logical hiding spots to hide the truth from man. But humans have large egos and love challenges. After many moons, they will eventually look to the highest mountains and find the means to go to the depths of the oceans, and one day they will discover truth. Humans always look outside themselves for truth, so I think the best place to hide it would be where they would never think to look—*inside* themselves."

They all laugh and agree that would be the best hiding place for truth, and they have left it there ever since.

Although the three gods of that story never anticipated it, a growing number of people *have* begun to look within themselves for the truth. We have begun to listen within for our own insight and wisdom through meditation, counseling, religion, prayer, reflection, and other forms of self-discovery. We want to discover for ourselves the truth of life and regain a feeling of hope and safety. We are beginning to discover that the answers we seek *do* lie within, from the voice of our true Selves. This voice of the true Self is the voice of wisdom, insight, common sense, and a higher perspective.

There are two courses one can take for this search within: the path of the ego/intellect and the path of the true Self. In the former, the ego attempts to look within by exploring belief systems, analyzing problems and issues, and relying on techniques in an effort to find something "to do." These mental gyrations keep the mind busy and under the illusion that it is making progress. However, as Einstein once said, "Imagination is more important than knowledge. For knowledge is limited, whereas imagination embraces the entire world, stimulating progress, giving birth to evolution." When we only look to our intellectual thought system and those of others, we are trapped by their inherent limitations.

The path of the true Self is about *truly* looking within—to the source of Universal Intelligence that lies within each human being. Inner truth is less concrete than what we are accustomed to thinking of as truth. It has low credibility in our ego-driven culture, and thus it is unfamiliar and unknown to most of us. That is why the gods hid it there. Nevertheless, if you are willing and open, you can begin to walk down this path. I will show you how. This path leads to a life without fear, and it is accessible to everyone.

The True Self

We come into this world of material form and creation from the world of the formless/spiritual, where there is no fear. And so as young children we are full of joy, curiosity, and a love of life. We are, by nature, fearless.

The longer we live in this world of material form, however, the more we forget about from what and where we came. And thus we mistakenly create a false sense of identity—our personality with all its habits—that we call the *ego*, which is Latin for "I." This ego identity feels separate from the Divine Source that birthed us, and we feel isolated, alone, and vulnerable. Thus we begin to live in fear. We identify with who we "think" we are: our labels (smart, poor, ugly, outgoing, artistic); our shortcomings (shy, uneducated, insecure); our possessions (house, car, toys); and our belief systems (religion, political party, liberal/conservative, optimist/pessimist).

The more afraid we are, the farther we move away from effortlessly being our true Selves, which we were closer to being when we were young children. A woman who was attending one of my seminars related a story of a three-year-old girl whose mother couldn't find her anywhere in the house. Finally, the mother discovered her little girl sitting on a bed with her new-born baby brother, who was taking a nap. At first the mother was afraid of what her little girl might do, but she quietly observed for a moment and overheard her three-year-old say to the infant, "Please tell me what God is like, because I am beginning to forget."

Like that little girl, we gradually forget where we came from. The result is an ever-present state of fear and insecurity. It naturally follows that we try to prove ourselves in order to gain respect, love, acceptance, and safety. In fact, most of us spend our entire lives trying to gain that love and security. We mistakenly believe that we can make ourselves safe by worrying and anticipating all the possible bad things that could befall us and then developing strategies to defeat them.

The true Self, this purest essence of who we are, knows no fear. The true Self knows it is one with life, that it is a part of a greater whole and thus has no enemies or competitors.

Our true Self is *one* with the Universal Intelligence that we often call God, the Higher Power, the Divine, the Great Spirit, Allah, the quantum field, or whatever name we choose. We are neither simply a by-product of It, nor are we just connected to It: we are a unique expression and individuation of the Infinite Beingness.

The problem with us as human beings is that we deny our oneness with this Universal Intelligence and look outside ourselves to a Being "up there." Once we create that false separation between the "I" of the ego and our Divine nature, we are on our own, so to speak, and have to look outside ourselves for redemption from some "other."

As a child I was taught the Judeo/Christian idea that God was "up there" (in the clouds or heaven) and that he was big with a long white beard. He was someone to be feared, since he was watching us all the time and he judged us for how we acted. No wonder I was afraid.

In the Book of Genesis, Adam and Eve were banished from the Garden of Eden (oneness with the Universal Intelligence) when they ate from the tree of knowledge and became aware of good and evil (the illusion of the separateness of all things, including ourselves). Like Adam and Eve, once we see the world in terms of good versus evil, us versus them—we have left the Garden of Eden and established the foundation of all conflict, disharmony with nature, violence, and war.

When we are our true Selves, we are back in the Garden of Eden. We are naturally relaxed, confident, wise, loveable, respectful, compassionate, loving, aware, and responsive to the moment. We see beauty in all of life and see solutions where others see impossibilities. We have answers to all of life's challenges and dilemmas, often in the form of simple wisdom. We receive that wisdom from Universal Intelligence in the form of knowing, instinct, intuition, gut feeling, insight, and inspiration.

We come to know that the truth is not stagnant. An insight from the Universal Intelligence/our true Self is responsive to each moment of our lives, giving us all we need to live fully.

As I go through my life I have challenges, obstacles, and issues to deal with, like any human being. However, when I feel angst, anxiety, or fear, I now know to look within and take time to ask my true Self questions that will give me answers from this inner intelligence and not from the limited awareness of my intellect/ego. For example, if I am stuck in my writing, I stop and take a moment to reflect on why I am stuck and then ask for a Divine viewpoint on my question. A practical and helpful answer usually comes quickly.

The Illusion of Separateness

Fear is the result of feeling separate from the Source that birthed and is one with our true Self. Our mothers symbolize this Source, but actually the Source is the Divine. When we feel separate from the Source of our true Self, we feel as vulnerable as a child would feel if deprived of its mother. We believe we must fend for ourselves, protect ourselves, defend ourselves from danger, and prove ourselves worthy of love and respect. This is the birth of the ego and our relationship with fear.

Unknowingly, we have chosen to be separate from our Source, though of course, separation is an impossibility, an illusion. We only *seem* to be separate. Nevertheless, the mind can create any thought—even the thought that we are separate—because we have free will. We can create the thought that we are unlovable, unworthy, bad, inferior, or superior, good, entitled—we can create any thought, true or untrue. Our free will to create thought and the resulting vivid experience is the most powerful gift we possess. We paint on the canvas of life, thus creating all the worlds in which we live. Without thought there would be no experience, but it is up to us how we use this gift of thought.

For example, we can create the thought that *nothing ever goes my way.* If we believe this thought, then we will interpret all subsequent information as supporting this assumption—either as a validation or an exception to the rule. Thus we create a self-fulfilling prophecy that *nothing goes my way and life is against me.* And if we don't recognize that thought as our free—will creation, we are trapped by the loop of thought → perception → interpretation → validation.

Thought Systems

The human mind organizes these thoughts, true or untrue, into a system of beliefs, opinions, conclusions, ideas, judgments, expectations, values, habits, and memories. This *thought system* is a self-fulfilling and self-validating system that acts like a filter through which the ego creates and views reality.

We each live in our own separate sphere created by the ego-based thought system. The more we believe in our limited, ego-based thought system and the less we listen to the boundless truth of our true Self, the more unhappy, fearful, and insecure we become. The more we cling to our ego-based thought system, the more isolated we feel from other human beings, and the more we tend to judge those who don't have a thought system that is similar to ours. Judgment, in turn, leads to hatred, violence, and ultimately war.

Misguided dependency on the ego and its thought system is the cause of all the problems we face in this world today. We feel trapped by our egos, prisoners of our own thought systems, and we desperately want to break out. What we don't realize is that we created our prison; we created our ego-based thought system, and ultimately we have the power to uncreate it and choose something else. We have the power to liberate ourselves by consciously choosing an awareness of who we truly are—not the self-created system of thoughts and personality traits that we call the ego, but rather the true Self that is an expression of the Divine Source, that is one with Universal Intelligence.

To live from our true Selves takes willingness, resolve, choice, courage, and acceptance. To live from our true Selves means giving up our addiction to the illusions of the external world and embracing the wisdom and truth of the world within.

We have set a misguided course for ourselves in life by making the unconscious choice to accept ourselves as less than our true Selves. In a sense, we have bought a ticket on a train of thought with a less than desirable (and sometimes horrifying) destination. Nevertheless, we feel confident that it is the right train, because almost everyone we know is a passenger. After all, most other people are worrying about the state of the world and about their personal lives. If we are not worrying along with them, then we must have missed the right train. Besides, the act of commiseration, our continual bonding with others over our fears and worries, is addictively satisfying.

It is not enough to acknowledge that we are headed in the wrong direction—that we are too fearful—and simply try to cope with being on that train. The course of the train is set, and if we stay on it we will stay in a state of fear. It was *our* previous choice to get on and stay on that train, unconscious as it may have been. We must now be *willing* to make a conscious choice to get off the train—and wake up to our true Selves. This is our only option to have a truly fearless life.

We cannot achieve liberation simply by practicing positive thinking. Positive thinking is inherently limited. Positive thinking assumes that there is something we have to *do* in order to cope with a negative reality, rather than seeing that it is our very *perception* of reality that is off. It is like staying on that same fearful train of thought but painting a fake scene on the train's windows so that the view appears to be different than it is. In other words, positive thinking puts a veneer over a negative view of life.

The kind of change I am proposing here is much more fundamental and deep—it doesn't just put another coat of paint on a negative world; it gets us to see a new world. It gets us off the old train of thought.

The Rumblings of Change

In these uncertain times, people are becoming disillusioned with our conventional institutions. While the world has reached unprecedented sophistication in the manipulation of public opinion, a backlash of people is obsessed with trying to uncover their hypocrisy. The media is debunking one leader after another and the organizations they belong to. *Collectively and unconsciously, we are trying to disillusion ourselves so that we may put trust within ourselves, not in an ego sense but in our true Self.* Only when we trust in our inner, higher authority—the true Self that is uncontaminated by the ego-based thought system—can we be truly free, safe, and fearless.

Paradoxically, it is only when we engage in this seemingly selfish act of completely trusting in ourselves that we connect to others in a profound way. In fact, when we discover our true Self and its oneness with Universal Intelligence, we see that everyone and everything is also one with that same Intelligence. We see the innocence of people who have forgotten this oneness and embraced the illusion of separateness, just as we did, and we don't pass judgment on them. We see the unity of all things and all beings. Discovering the true Self and living from it is the key to living a fearless life. For how can we fear that which is one with ourselves?

Why Are We So Afraid?

When we are disconnected from our true Selves, we see the world as made up of those we can trust and those we can't. The illusion of separateness gives rise to the fear-based mentality of us versus them. Once we adopt fear as our stance in this world, we are destined to see others and the world defensively and as a threat. We see people in black-and-white categories of good and bad, right and wrong, crazy and sane, left wing and right wing, friend and foe. This is the kind of thinking that leads to political deadlock, division, racism, sexism, terrorism, war, greed, and economic injustice.

Until we are aware of and trust our true Selves instead of our ego-based thought system, we will not trust others, nor will we be able to see through to the truth when *they* are deceived by their own thinking. But as we begin to gain awareness of our true Self and trust the voice of our wisdom, as we begin to live our lives from the stance of love, rather than fear, we begin to see that life is full of abundance, help, guidance, opportunities, adventure, wonder, and awe. Love and wisdom begin to guide our every move, decision, and interaction with others. We feel a sense of unity with others and see our common values, purpose, and universal source. We feel eternal hope.

We also see how to be safe in this world in a very common-sense way, without limiting our capacity for joy and enjoyment of our lives. Being our true Selves does not mean we live in the oblivion of "la la land." On the contrary, when we live from our true Selves we have a heightened and wise sense of awareness and perception of how to live safely.

Reclaiming the True Self

Can you learn to be your true Self? *You can't learn to be your true Self, because the true Self already exists.* There is nothing to learn about it—you have only to discover and experience the truth about who you are. For millennia, experts, authorities, and religious leaders have been trying to tell us to look to them or to their belief systems for the source of truth. But the truth can only be found in one place—within each of us.

A few years ago I got a call from a rabbi in Jerusalem after he had read my book, *The Serenity Principle.* He is a scholar of the Torah, the most sacred of the Jewish scriptures, and has spent his lifetime trying to understand the essence of its message. He explained to me that the ideas of my book were the same as the unspeakable truths contained in the Torah. For me this is proof that truth is universal, and at the same time extremely personal. Our limited use of language can never fully explain truth—it can only point us to it so that we may have our own experience. As the Hindus say, "The finger pointing to the moon is not the moon, it can only direct the eyes to see for themselves."

Seeing truth is an inner experience, not a conceptual idea, so be patient and listen with your heart as you read the words that follow. Remember as you read to look for an *experience* that comes in the form of a feeling. Like a welcome, invisible wind that cools you on a hot summer day, your experience of the truth transcends words.

"Looking within" has become a cliché whose meaning often eludes us. When I speak here of looking within, I am not talking about looking to our intellectual system of preconceived beliefs and trying to figure out our problems. Quite the contrary; analyzing will only block our ability to look within.

What I am talking about when I speak of looking within is quieting the intellectual mind and creating a space for the voice of our true Self to speak through insight and revelation. Common examples of looking within are contemplation, reflection, "putting a problem on the back burner," or having an insight upon awakening, while exercising, or while doing some other calming activity.

We each will discover our own route to this inner sanctuary of truth.

Where Do We Look When We Look Within?

"Within" is not a physical place, such as the heart or the brain. *"Within" is a state of Being.* Being just *is.*

At our core we are this Being state. Because this state is invisible, it is difficult to describe, yet it is the essential creative force behind our lives. It has been called consciousness, the soul, the "I am." *Being* is an inner treasure that contains all of our dreams, our heart's desires, our true purpose, and genius—all that we long for and all that we have not yet begun to long for.

Being is not born of the limited thoughts of the ego self; it is the unlimited true Self, which is one with Universal Intelligence. We have all felt the experience of Being our true Selves in very ordinary circumstances—when we see beauty, feel love for a child, experience contentment, fall in love, or come up with a creative idea that no one has thought of before. We feel powerful and connected with all creation, we feel loving and complete when we touch our Being within, even if only for a brief moment.

For most of my life I was sure these moments had to do with the people I was with, the beauty of the nature around me, or the song I was inspired by. I had no idea that the experience of these precious moments was coming from *me,* from my true Self. These moments were so different from the ordinary experiences of my personality that I thought they must be coming from the outside, and thus I tried to recreate those moments by repeating the external circumstances. The joy from these externals was fleeting and unpredictable. Later I was to realize that the experience of my true Self is so distinctly different from the ego self that it was no wonder I didn't know how to recognize it. This insight left me open and gave me resolve to uncover my true Self.

Most of us search all our lives for these brief moments of connection to Being. We feel safe, secure, and that all is well. We access this Beingness when we are *present*—not caught up in our normal fearful state of anxiety, stress, worry, and other unpleasant emotions. When our thoughts clear, like clouds parting in the sky, our Beingness is revealed—the eternal sun shines.

Going within to our treasure house of Beingness is natural, though it may initially feel awkward, even troubling, because the ego self's habit of being fearful has become an addiction. And like most addicts, those of us who are addicted to fear (to varying degrees) don't think we have a problem. Being fearful simply feels normal to us, just as drinking feels normal to an alcoholic or smoking feels normal to a smoker.

Our addiction to fear is actually much more difficult for us to see as harmful than the addiction to drinking or drugs or smoking. Society continually tells us that alcoholism, drug abuse, and smoking are unacceptable. But no one tells us that living in fear is unacceptable, nor will anyone tell us that we are in denial of our addiction to it. On the contrary, living in fear is totally acceptable to most people, and giving it up would be seen as being in denial of the ever-present dangers in our world.

And so, like a drug addict that becomes used to the life of urges → preoccupation → pursuit → fix → satiation → urges, we too get used to lives of fear—worry, stress, tension, apprehension, boredom, impatience—they are all part of normal, everyday life. We see relaxing and letting down our guard as something we reserve for vacation time and brief moments, but not for "normal life."

The emotion of fear has become such a habit that many seek out circumstances to feel more fear. Adrenaline junkies become addicted to gambling, shoplifting, extreme sports, sexual affairs, or high-risk situations like stock trading primarily for the rush that comes with the fear.

I recently heard a radio interview with a woman who worked in a bar as the cash ticket person. Over time she began to steal small amounts of money each day, at first because she felt her employer was not paying her enough, but eventually for the rush of the risk of being caught. She eventually stole up to a thousand dollars a night and would run to her car late at night in a seamy neighborhood, having parked her car in increasingly dicey locations in order to flirt even more with danger. She even rationalized that God was helping her. In return, she would give generous donations to her church each Sunday to pay God his share. She later confessed that it was the rush of fear she was addicted to, not the money.

My Search

For most of my life I have wrestled with the same questions that plague us as a people. My search for answers has paid off in the richest of ways, for it forced me to see that truth was not to be found outside myself. Instead, I discovered my true Self, wherein lies true meaning and a peaceful life.

I feel a deep love for humanity and the planet and have a strong feeling of love for my wife, my family, and my friends. I am at peace in this world that is in chaos by most people's assessment. I have found that a life of fearlessness is not only more enjoyable, it is also safer, healthier, freer, more abundant, and more loving.

How is this possible? Skeptical minds might assume denial, delusion, drugs, or dropping out. But I have not dropped out of society, nor have I quit reading the newspaper or moved to a cave on the mountaintops of the Himalayas. I am fully engaged in the world, but I have found a deep sense of peace and joy that I never imagined was likely here on Earth.

What I have found is so simple yet so profound that it is worth writing a book about. In short, I have discovered how to live from my true Self in this world. I have discovered and experienced the nature of the core of my being—security, oneness with others, love, peace of mind, purposefulness, joy, and a deep knowing that all is well. I have discovered how to be *in* this world but not *of* it.

Being in the World but Not of It

What I mean by being *in* the world but not *of* it is the crux of this book. Being in the world but not of it means that instead of reacting to the world around us from fear and our ego-based thought system, we respond to the world from the source of our true Selves, from love. When we respond to the world from a place of love, we act in a manner that is nonreactive, wise, creative, and safe.

Being in the world but not of it is a way of being that allows us to be active, engaged, and involved in the world without being at the mercy of circumstances, events, and other people's moods, actions, and judgments toward us. *We live in the world, but we are not defined by it. We know that there is a deeper place that transcends the external world, and that deeper place is our true Self. Thus we live in the world, but we are of the true Self.* This profound realization allows us to live in a state of immunity from the world and its many sources of negativity.

As we explore the distinction between the true Self and the false self we call the ego, we learn that the only antidote to fear is a return to the true Self. When we return to the true Self, we rediscover the ease with which we can live our lives, especially in these times of terrorist threats, ecological and climatic crises, economic uncertainty, and rapid social and technological change. In a sense, living from our core Self forms the bedrock of living lives that are safe, secure, free, and full of joy, purpose, and connection to others.

REMINDERS

1. We terrorize ourselves with our own thoughts, innocently unaware that we are the creators of our own fear.
2. Once we realize that the essence of who we are is the boundless true Self—not the limited set of personality traits, habits, and beliefs that make up the false self we call the ego—we are free to create the life we want.
3. Discovering the true Self within is the antidote to fear addiction.
4. Our true nature is spiritual.

CHAPTER 4
Creators of Experience

We are the creators of our experience. We all go through life, day after day, thinking, choosing, declaring, believing, and interpreting all the content and events of our very existence. Most of the time we are creating our experience completely out of the view of our conscious mind. We are "thinking" behind the scenes, and that thinking dictates our perceptions, interpretations, emotions, and our actions—indeed our whole life. For most of us, this unconscious thinking creates a life of fear, stress, worry, and dissatisfaction.

Every now and then we wake up and realize, *I am making this all up in my mind.* However, these enlightened moments are few and far between for the average person.

Just last night I was having dinner with a friend who is a nationally recognized expert in global warming. As I listened to his litany of frightening scenarios about our planet, I lost my bearings for a moment and began to feel hopeless, fearful, and overwhelmed. I felt a sickening feeling in the pit of my stomach, which woke me up to the fact that I was losing conscious awareness of my thinking and my emotional reactions. I felt caught in an all too familiar quandary—I want to be informed and to do what I can to prepare my own family and my community, but I don't want to panic or live in fear. Then, by noticing the feeling in my stomach and my hopelessness, I remembered, *I am creating my own experience. Do I want to do it from my fear-based ego or from my true*

Self's core of wisdom and hope? This simple realization allowed me to rechoose my experience. I regained my perspective, calmed down, and saw what I could change in my world and what I needed to let go of.

I feel extremely fortunate that I am aware of the difference between my ego tricking me into fear and my true Self leading the way into my experience of life. You too can find this freedom, once you gain an understanding of how we create experience, and once you are willing to let go of the habits of the ego self.

What if we were to wake up every day and consistently realize that *we are the authors of our experience?* What if we were to live and think consciously? What if we were to choose our lives based on our reflections and the Universal Intelligence from our true Self rather than from the habits of our ego-based thought system? What if we were to live our lives from truth?

We all have this capability available to us if we are willing, open, and take the time to listen to our true Selves. It is our choice, *once we become aware.*

In this chapter we explore our power to create an individual, self-created reality, and thus increase our awareness of this process. Our conscious and unconscious thoughts and choices create our reality from moment to moment. We have a choice to create our reality either from the fear-based ego thought system or from our spiritual essence—the true Self. We can discover how to translate this understanding into a process for breaking our addiction to fear.

How We Create

Almost without notice, we go through our day making various declarations: *I am so lazy! I am so overwhelmed with my life; I'll never catch up. Life is so hard! I am so fat, ugly, dumb, crazy, nervous, scared, weird, stressed.* Whatever we say to ourselves through our thinking is the blueprint for our reality. Whatever we believe at our core is what we experience and what happens to us in life. This incessant inner rambling is the voice of the ego, completely unaware that it is living in a delusion of self-generated thought.

Most of my life I had no idea whatsoever that I was the creator of my reality. I was taught and believed wholeheartedly that my life came from "out there"—from other people (parents, teachers, my mate, someone at school); from situations and events (the weather, the traffic, my work circumstances, how much I weighed, how much money I had, events in the world); and from my past (how I had been wronged, the successes or failures I had experienced, living up to my and others' expectations). It appeared as though my life was the sum total of what I had been handed in terms of genetics, opportunities, parents, family, schools I had attended, and situations I found myself in. I often felt sorry for myself, for I was a victim of life. Sometimes I felt superior to others in terms of my accomplishments, my values, my actions, my looks, or possessions. I lived in a world of continually comparing myself to others, of constantly judging myself and others based on my own and others' expectations.

This was the world of the ego—judging, analyzing, striving, expecting, and consequently feeling guilty or stressed. I had no idea that I had created all of this with my unconscious thinking. Of course, I had help from my family, my peers, and society in general, but *I* had written the script from the various possibilities presented to me. I was responsible!

Once I began to realize this, at the age of thirty-three, I felt foolish, relieved, free, and innocent. Once I realized that I had been *innocently* creating all my feelings and experiences—joy, sadness, anger, stress, happiness, all of them—I felt empowered and forgiving of myself. I realized the power of thought to create my experience and the power to *choose* my life, no longer from the limitations of my ego, but from the limitless Self that is my Spirit and the essence of all of us.

Don't Believe Everything You Think

When I woke up to the fact that I was the creator of my experience through my thinking and my choices, I was freed from my prison of thought. I still spent a lot of time in my prison cell, but I *knew* the door wasn't locked. Whenever I remember that I am in the prison of habitual thinking, I am free to rechoose my experience simply by being aware that I am the creator, the thinker, and the chooser of my life. This simple awareness has changed my life from one of fear and stress to one of peace of mind and clarity of thinking.

This is a power we all have—to create our lives, to think whatever we choose, and to act on whatever thoughts we choose to engage in and fuel. One of my favorite bumper stickers reads "Don't Believe Everything You Think." Just because a thought comes into our mind, it doesn't mean it is true, worthy of our attention, or wise.

Every day, many irrelevant, unwise, false, and harmful thoughts come into my mind—mostly from past conditioning. Lots of wise, helpful, loving, and intelligent thoughts also come into my mind. Regardless of what comes into my mind, I know that seated in the middle of all those thoughts is *me*—my conscious awareness, my power of discernment, the observer, the witness, my true Self. There I sit in the middle of all my thinking, free to decide what thoughts to listen to, ignore, act on, reflect on, put on the back burner, fantasize about, tell to others, forget, accept, deny, and many more reactions to my thoughts.

I am free. And so are *you*.

The Power of the Phrase "I Am"

I am. It is such a simple phrase. I am. Whatever follows that phrase is my *creation*.

I am happy. *I am* sad. *I am* hopeful. *I am* depressed. *I am* scared. *I am* lucky. *I am.* . . . You fill in the blank and you deem it so.

As Divine Beings we are privileged to create our lives, one thought at a time. If only we awake and remember that we are the dreamer of our dreams, our nightmares, our hopes, and our expectations, we see that the whole creation is ours.

I am. Two simple yet powerful words lead to the act of creation. Think of that! Isn't that amazing? It *is* amazing, and it is even more amazing to remember it in the moment-to-moment existence of our lives. This is the power of *awareness*.

Being aware of the fact that we are an integral part of the creation of our reality and our world allows us to use our free will consciously. Without consciousness, we are victims of our past conditioning. We must realize that *we are conditioned, but we are not our conditioning,* just as we can choose to be *in* the world but not *of* the world. We get to choose whether or not to grant power to our conditioned thoughts.

I am is the most powerful tool of creation there is. The *I* is the energy, the source, and the author. The *am* is the release of this spiritual power into the world of form, the world of the senses. The *am* is like the light switch—illuminating the thoughts and beliefs we want to empower.

Creating from Separation (Ego) or the True Self

Many thoughts that we carry with us—many of which are unconscious thoughts—are remnants of past choices we have made. For example, as a child I watched my parents worry about all kinds of things—the family business, money, their children, the economy, the weather, and what was on the news. From watching their behavior, I assumed that worry was just what human beings did much of the time. I had no idea that worry was a choice or might be optional. So I became a worrier, and when I became a parent I worried even more. I thought it was part of my job. I didn't consciously think this or decide this; it just never occurred to me to think otherwise. Nonetheless, worrying was a choice I had made.

All of us carry around beliefs born of our unconscious choices each day. These beliefs and choices affect many of our daily decisions and the quality of our lives, yet we have no idea we are doing this. I think of the unconscious influence of our socialization as like living under a power line. It is constantly emitting electrical energy, but it is doing so invisibly and out of our conscious awareness. Nonetheless it is having a long-term effect on our lives.

I do not wish to suggest that it is wise to simply "recondition" our old thoughts with new thoughts. When we exchange thoughts with other thoughts, even if they are more positive, wiser, or of a higher value, we are still creating from the ego self. Much has been written about positive thinking, affirmations, reprogramming our thoughts, thought control, rational thinking, goal attainment, and a host of other New Age and pop psychology approaches. Although these approaches are effective in changing our thinking and our behavior temporarily, we always end up with a new set of problems that still do not lead us to happiness and true peace of mind, or we tire of the rituals and revert back to our old habits. This is because these approaches are born of the limited and separated state of the ego self.

Only the pure thoughts of the true Self are born of Divinity and therefore are in harmony with all people and all things. Thoughts born of the ego self often lead to greed, disharmony, and self-centeredness with nature and other human beings. In the world of ego there is never enough—power, money, love, possessions, security, information, or pleasure. When we operate from the true Self, our thinking is wise, intelligent, and grounded in the Universal Intellect. It has access to all that is in our memory but also to intuition, creative thought, and insights, plus the ability to pull them all together in a responsive way to create a safe and beautiful life. With all that abundance, we live in a state of bounty and gratitude.

When we become aware of the voice of our true Self, we hear thoughts that come from pure consciousness—thoughts that are Divine in nature. Pure thought and pure consciousness stem from *Being*—our true nature. *We are Divine by nature.*

Though the thoughts of the little ego mind seem to dominate our thinking, the still, small voice of the true Self is always there, whispering the truth to us. When we pause, reflect, and listen within, we hear its constant wisdom. Like a deep well, whenever we dip down into the wisdom of the true Self, it refreshes, renews, and restores us. It reassures us to know the well is there, but we must choose to dip into it. We must turn within and trust ourselves. When we do, our fears subside and our minds become quiet and calm. In this silence, we find the pure consciousness that we have sought all our lives; thoughts that are wise, encouraging, truthful, and honest come to us.

Sometimes human beings experience this still, small voice of wisdom when the ego thought system is temporarily "put to sleep." For example, during a crisis or in life-threatening situations, some people report a deep sense of calm, a moment of clarity in which they are able to respond to the situation with great speed and intelligence. Others may experience this wisdom on vacation, in nature, while exercising, or during deep states of meditation. However, unless you understand the principles involved, you have to wait for another circumstance to trigger this state of natural consciousness.

How, you might wonder, can you make these unusual situations more accessible? The first step is learning how to tell the difference between your contaminated thought system and the voice of the true Self.

Emotional Guidance

When we create our reality from ego and past habits, we may experience uncomfortable feelings, such as anxiety, stress, resentment, anger, guilt, regret, depression, dread, apprehension, and a host of other negative emotions. We may also experience more pleasurable feelings, such as excitement, superiority, relief, a sense of accomplishment, pride, and satisfaction. The ego can create positive and negative emotions, but they are all dependent on external events, accomplishments, or other people's responses to us. If it is a sunny day we are happy; if it rains, we are sad. If you act the way I want you to I feel happy; if you don't I feel disappointed. If the stock market goes up, I feel secure; if it goes down, I feel scared.

When we create our reality from our Divine thoughts and Divine consciousness, we experience deep, positive, powerful feelings. These feelings don't depend on externals, but are simply a function of our state of mind. No matter what the weather, the current world situation, other people's moods, or our bank account balance, we feel an internal sense of joy and well-being when we create from the true Self.

Figure 4 indicates the directional nature of our sensations and emotions.

All emotions are the biochemical result of a thought or series of thoughts in our brain. Through the link of our neurotransmitters, our thoughts, and neuropeptides, we create a cascade of emotions with each series of associative thoughts. As such, emotions are a feedback mechanism informing us of the proper use of our thinking and behavior. If we are aware of emotions as a feedback mechanism instead of just feeling like we are under their power, we can then ask ourselves, "where is the emotion coming from, our true Self, or our ego?" We must trust that the internal, Universal Intelligence is guiding us, through the sensations of our emotions, back to our true Self. Simply shining the light of awareness on our emotions and observing them without judg-

Figure 4 THE EMOTIONAL GUIDANCE SYSTEM

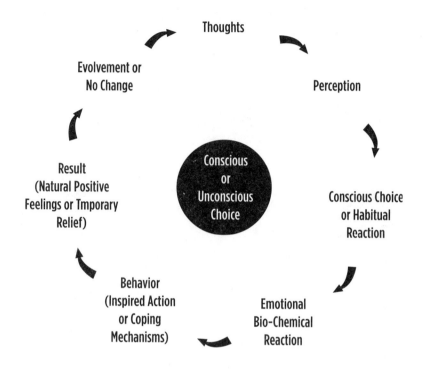

ment is sufficient to return us to a calm, serene mind. *Awareness without judgment* of what we are feeling reconnects us to our true Selves and the wisdom that comes with it.

Oprah Faces Her Fears

Recently, Oprah did a series of shows on fear for her daily TV show as well as for her O magazine. One of the specials was on the bird flu pandemic: how real is the danger, what we can do to prepare, and how we should respond. As the infectious disease expert presented the facts, the catastrophic scenarios, and how unprepared we are as a society for such a real possibility, Oprah looked more and more concerned, as were many in the audience. She finally said to the expert, "I am feeling really hopeless, frightened, and overwhelmed by this information and you are speaking about only one of the many possible disasters we now face in the world. Please tell me something to give me hope." The doctor responded by talking about what people could do to prepare, such as contacting their legislators, stockpiling food and water supplies, and buying air purification masks. He didn't respond to her fear, her state of being, just the practical things she and everyone could do, which was his area of expertise. I could sense Oprah's despair and the overwhelmed feeling of the audience. As I listened, I too experienced some of that same fear and despair.

However, my feelings very quickly changed from fear and despair to calm and hope, because I have built up a strong mental immunity to the fears of the world. As a physical immune system allows us to withstand exposure to viruses, a mental immune system allows us to face harmful thoughts with a sense of balanced awareness and calm. How did I build up this immunity? Through the ongoing practice of the transformational process that I describe next.

Say I am watching a cable TV news show or editorial commentary. One of the pundits makes a statement that triggers a flurry of reactive thoughts. Perhaps this is the intent of the show, to provoke a reaction, whether it is from the left- or right-wing commentator. If I begin to feel fear, outrage, anger, or despair, that is information for me to observe from a stance of deep listening. I might think, *That's interesting that I am having such a strong reaction.* I am not discounting my reaction, I am simply becoming *curious* about it. From the stance of curiosity about my reaction, I am able to reflect so that I can consciously *choose* how to respond: from my true Self or from my ego.

If I begin to react with outrage and judgment, the sensation in my body is negative and uncomfortable. These feelings are also information and guidance. Therefore, I might ask myself, *Do I want to entertain these outraged, judgmental thoughts? Is the state-*

ment *I'm reacting to relevant to my life? Is there anything I want to do about it?* I might see my reaction as having nothing directly to do with the situation but a response to an old belief that it is now time to reveal. I am confronted with *the power of choice*—the choice to be outraged, the choice to continue watching or not, the choice to act on my emotions, or the choice to reflect on their relevance to my life.

Whatever the situation in our lives, we are free to react or not react. We are free to respond from our wisdom, or from fear and reactivity. The TV doesn't get to decide for us—we are the choosers of our reactions and what we do with our reactions. The simple act of *noticing the quality of our experience* can enable us to get back on the path of our true Selves and live our lives fearlessly. If we choose fear, that will take us down one path (the limited world of the ego). If we choose peace and fearlessness, that will take us down a very different path (the boundless path of the true Self). Choosing fearlessness allows us to see what we can do and what we can't, how involved to be or not, whether to act or withdraw. This is the path of wisdom.

The Process of Breaking Our Addiction to Fear

Once we are aware that fear and worry come from the ego self, we need not chastise ourselves for having indulged in those habits. On the contrary, simply being aware of our fear—without judgment—is enough for our Divine Intelligence to come into action and transform our fear into calm. Transforming our thinking, emotions, and behavior occurs naturally through the process of being aware of those thoughts and emotions and taking a nonjudgmental stance toward them.

In fact, if we deny that we are worried or afraid or judge ourselves for feeling that way, these emotions will leave our awareness and become projected on others and events of our lives.

Projection occurs when our emotions are denied, and as a result, our thought habits become unconscious. Then, our thoughts act like an invisible filter that obscures reality with prejudiced interpretation. It is only when we accept *all* feelings as fleeting thoughts that don't control us that they move through us and transform into the balance we seek.

Our Divine Intelligence, our true Self, is like a pilot light that is always on, ready to ignite the power of awareness and insight, whenever called on, and thus empower us to transform to our true nature. This Divine Intelligence is the *default setting* that kicks in whenever we let go of our attachment to harmful thinking and feeling. We must simply accept our humanness, accept that we all feel fear from time to time, and let go of the thinking that recreates old habitual patterns of thought. When we do this and then turn to our inner wisdom by reflecting and asking questions, our Divine Intelligence shows up in the form of insights. I talk about this process in detail later in the book, in chapter 6.

This process of increasing awareness is ongoing; we will never arrive at a point of knowing it all. Rather, we will perpetually be moving into the unknown and discovering more of our limitless Self.

In the case of watching Oprah's show on bird flu, I unconsciously began to react fearfully to the very educational show on the possibility of a future pandemic. As my emotions and thoughts came into my awareness and I observed them without judgment, my feelings returned to a state of equilibrium. By being aware of what I was feeling without judging, or needing to go into denial about the whole topic, I was able to make a choice to not get caught up in fear. Prior to this understanding I would have reacted as most people do—either becoming panicked or going into denial. The alternative approach looks something the circle presented in Figure 5.

Creating Our Experience from the True Self

When we create experience from our true Selves we do it without any effort, we do it fearlessly, and we create more intelligently. We may call this experience creativity, inspiration, genius, out of the blue thoughts, insights, being in the zone, or a state of grace. Most of us have had moments of this experience, caught glimpses of it, or witnessed it in others, such as athletes, performers, public speakers, spiritual leaders, and young children. Though these moments seem rare and unusual, they are totally natural when we are living and creating from the true Self.

There is nothing we can *do* to make our true Self appear, for we *are* the true Self, and nothing can ever destroy that fact—we can only cover up our awareness of it in the moment through

Figure 5 CREATING OUR EXPERIENCE FROM THE TRUE SELF

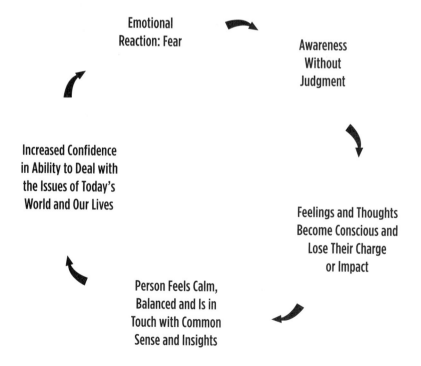

Emotional Reaction: Fear

Awareness Without Judgment

Increased Confidence in Ability to Deal with the Issues of Today's World and Our Lives

Feelings and Thoughts Become Conscious and Lose Their Charge or Impact

Person Feels Calm, Balanced and Is in Touch with Common Sense and Insights layers of ego-based thought. When we are aware that we are caught up in our ego-based thinking, we needn't *do* anything. We simply observe. We don't judge or analyze the thinking. We accept and forgive ourselves for the thoughts. We open ourselves to uncovering something deeper. Like magic, we automatically begin to move into a state of release from those thoughts. The awareness is enough to transform the fear into perspective. This automatic transformation feels magical, but it is as simple as the touching of a hot radiator; when I remove my hand, it quits burning almost immediately.

This process makes way for an experience of our true Self. It may begin with a feeling of letting go, relief, calm. And then we open our minds and hearts to a new experience of thoughts and feelings derived from the Being of Self. Just knowing that at our core we are that Spirit, that Universal Intelligence, allows it to come more into our conscious awareness. In this sense, it is our default setting. Our true Self is our natural Self.

REMINDERS

1. We are the creators of our experience.
2. We are able to create consciously or unconsciously.
3. Awareness of the process of creation empowers us to experience our free will.
4. "I am" is the power of creation in action.
5. We are free to create from the ego self or the true Self.
6. Emotions are the guidance system that allows us to become aware of whether we are creating from the ego self or the true Self.
7. Awareness of our fears and worries without judgment or effort leads to their transformation into a state of calm.

CHAPTER 5
Choice
THE INSTRUMENT OF CREATION AND THE ESSENCE OF SAFETY

As human beings, we have the awesome power to create for ourselves fearproof lives. That power is the power of choice. Choice is the instrument of creation that allows us to act on our free will. We can use our free will to choose to live from our true Selves. Or we can choose to stay in the prison of the ego self. We can choose to align with the true Self's wisdom and protection. Or we can choose to live in the grip of fear.

The popular science fiction trilogy *The Matrix* illustrates our dilemma with choice. In this story, the world of the Matrix is actually an illusionary reality created by machines. Humans operate inside a machine-programmed mental holograph. None of what they see is real, but rather is an illusion that appears real. Unbeknownst to most, humans are confined in a coma state, electrically connected to the machines, while inside their minds they "live" in the machine-created illusion they call reality. A few people escape this illusion and "choose to go down the rabbit hole," thus discovering what is real and what is illusion, which is the key to true Self-knowledge. In classic Hollywood fashion, the story is also a war between good and evil, with the machines exemplifying evil and the human protagonist Neo exemplifying good.

In the first movie of the trilogy, Neo has to choose his fate—either to continue living in the fake, machine-created world or to see that world for what it is: an illusion. Neo discovers that he is "the one" who is supposed to help set everyone free. Like Neo, we face a similar choice: Do we leave the false security of the known, ego-created illusionary world for the unknown of the true Self's real world? Do we choose to let go of our fear and leave the familiar boundaries of our thought system and our ego for the limitlessness of our true Self?

This is the choice that we must all make. If we choose to live in the illusion of our conditioned thought system, we can go on believing we are making choices from the box of illusion. Or we can venture *inside* to the world of unlimited choice and freedom in the realm of the true Self. Choosing from our true Self is the only *true* freedom.

The Key to Freedom from Addiction

Most of my life I made choices unconsciously, based on the conditioned patterns of thought that I had acquired from my family, my environment, and my life experiences. In making unconscious choices I became a prisoner of my own thinking, which was limited to what I thought was possible, what I thought I deserved, and what I believed was "normal." It was only when I began to understand that my own limited thinking created my limited reality that I chose to calm my mind and open up to the wondrous possibilities of a life lived from my true Self. Now I feel a freedom from fear and worry that I never imagined possible.

Do you want to be free? Do you want to make choices that are your own, that come from your spiritual nature, and not those that have been handed down by well-meaning but misguided institutions, individuals, and ideas of our current culture? If so, read on and discover the power of choice in your life.

Conscious and Unconscious Thought

Each day thousands of thoughts pass through our minds. Some thoughts are born of association; we hear someone say something and it reminds us of something we already know. We instantly connect these two thoughts, forming an illusionary conclusion that we believe we accurately heard what the other person said. Our habitual, ego-based thoughts act like a filter that obscures our hearing and all our senses.

Occasionally, we are relaxed enough to actually hear what the other person is saying. It is only through an awareness of which of these sources of thought is in operation (the ego or the true Self) that we experience the freedom of choice: limited habit or boundless wisdom. Otherwise we may be choosing, but we are doing so from the unconscious blindness of the ego.

In order to act on our free will and use the power of choice to create a life from our true Selves, we must discover how to remain conscious. We must make our choices based on the thoughts that come from our fully conscious true Self. It is only when we live from the true Self that we can break our addiction to fear. How do we do this?

The Power of Choice

We create our world through the power of choice. Every moment we are choosing, thinking, and creating our world, whether we know it or not. We are conscious, thinking Beings, imbued with the power to create every emotion, perception, action, and experience of our lives. How can we use this power of choice to consciously create harmony in our lives? And how can we avoid using it unconsciously, thus doing harm to ourselves, others, and the world in which we live?

What is choice? We use the word quite freely every day, but what does it really mean? *Choice is using the power of mind to create something out of nothing.* It is using the invisible energy of the spiritual Source that we all are connected to and a part of, to manifest from the world of the formless to the world of form. Each time we are aware of a possibility of choice, we can either choose from our ego state or choose from our true Self. We can choose from unconscious habits or from the wisdom of our spiritual essence.

For example, I may imagine that I would like to learn something new, like a new language, a computer program, or how to play a musical instrument. If fear kicks in and I entertain that feeling, I may have thoughts like, *I'm too old to learn a language.* Or, *I never have been very musical; what makes me think I'll be able to play an instrument now?* Or, *I really don't have time for anything else in my life; I'm already overwhelmed.* All of these thoughts, if I choose to take them seriously, would torpedo my budding, heartfelt desire and diminish my life.

If I ignore the fearful, self-sabotaging thoughts and stay open to the possibility of *discovery*, I would begin to notice many possibilities to manifest that budding dream. Perhaps I might see a piece in a newsletter about an upcoming class on the computer program I want to learn. Or I meet someone who tutors people in the language I want to learn. When we are operating from our secure, true Self, we start seeing possibilities and potential choices.

At each fork in the road of possibility, we will always be confronted with two choices: fear or openness. If I take the path of fear, I will stay stuck in the secure, familiar, small world of the ego. If I choose the path of openness, I will be able to listen within to see if the opportunity that presents itself is the one I want to pursue from the infinite set of possibilities.

In my own life, I did hire that Spanish tutor and am having a ball learning a language. I even formed a Spanish club with friends and family who share the same dream. Our lives are enhanced and more fun!

Choosing from Ego or Choosing from Our True Self

Early on in our lives, most of us unknowingly chose to identify with our beliefs, memories, and habits—our egos. As we learned and accepted a limited view of ourselves based on others' opinions of us and our own conclusions, we created an identity based on these beliefs. Seeing ourselves in this limited way led many of us to make the rest of our choices in life based on our limited belief systems rather than on the unlimited wisdom of our true Self. "That's just the way I am, that's my personality." Whenever we make choices from the separated state of the ego, we inevitably make choices that take us out of balance with ourselves, each other, and the world around us. It is no wonder that so many human beings live lives of fear, unhappiness, boredom, and discontent. In my own life, as I became an adult I became increasingly serious, heavy hearted, and stressed. I lost the lighthearted innocence of my youth and the capacity to see beauty and unlimited possibilities.

The good news is that we all have the power to *rechoose* our lives. We can *rechoose* to live wholeheartedly from our true Selves. In so doing, we set in motion a new level of awareness of the infinite set of choices that come from the abundance of possibilities within each of us. This process may begin with our recognizing that we are stuck in our habitual belief system and choosing not to accept it. If we then choose "the other"—that is, our true Self— we will be open to discover what comes to mind. We will begin to develop an ear for when a thought is coming from the limited ego self or if it has the ring of truth and wisdom that is characteristic of our true Self.

As discussed in the last chapter, we start to listen to the guidance system of our feelings, which lets us know where we are coming from—from fear or from love. Each time we have a thought and begin to entertain it as a reality or possibility, the thought triggers a chain reaction of cascading chemical reactions called emotions. These emotions, in turn, trigger associations to our memories, further reinforcing the emotional reaction. As a result, our thoughts and feelings can begin to spin out of control. As this happens, our awareness level drops and we *project* our out-of-control thoughts onto the circumstances we are in.

The key is to recognize the quality of our emotions. Recognizing the quality of our emotions enables us to enter the state of *the observer*—an objective awareness of our moment-to-moment use of thought. In other words, we regain consciousness and are able to pull back from our emotional reactions and thoughts.

Each choice we make from this aware state of the observer gives us additional feedback on the quality of the results of our choices. This observer state is emotionally neutral; it is objective. Thus it helps us to hone in on the power we have of making wiser and more intelligent choices. The more we make conscious choices that are in alignment with our true Selves, the more we realize the magnitude of our power as creators. As we do this, we return to our childlike view of the world—fresh and awe inspiring, but with the experience and knowledge base that comes from living our lives in the world.

When we realize our power to choose our experience, we no longer feel overwhelmed and powerless when watching the cable news or, for that matter, confronting any event in our lives.

Initially, when we become aware that we have a choice, we must be careful not to fill our heads with our preconceived notions of what we *believe* would be a wise choice. Instead, we simply choose not to accept the old habit and leave some space for a new idea to enter. Thus we allow some room for the unknown to do its work. Eventually, thoughts of wisdom will begin to flow to us naturally.

Figure 6 illustrates this process.

The Observer

In the 1960s the renowned Canadian brain surgeon Wilder Penfield conducted numerous experiments in which he mapped out the brain, determining the localization of such functions as sight, touch, cognitive abilities, and hearing. In hundreds of brain surgeries he would electrically stimulate every part of his

Figure 6 THRIVING FEARLESSLY

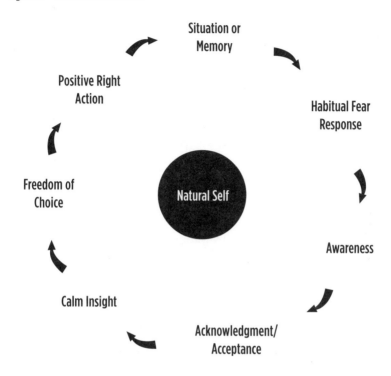

patients' brains while they were conscious and have them report their experiences. Thus he discovered that each patient would report the same type of experiences when the same area of the brain was stimulated. Although his experiments provided a tremendous advancement in the new science of brain function, he was never able to stimulate the areas of the brain responsible for self-awareness and decision making. He was never able to resolve this dilemma. Self-awareness and the capacity to choose, he concluded, lay in a realm outside of the body.

As a psychologist and psychotherapist, I found his conclusions fascinating, because the two functions of awareness and choice are essential to mental health and the ability of my patients to have insights about themselves and make choices that change the course of their lives. Yet, these functions are not located in our conditioned thought system. They do not reside in our memories, our ability to analyze, to think, to remember, to hypothesize, or to experience perception and emotions (the brain). Where, I wondered, could these abilities reside? As I studied many religions of the world and learned meditation, I discovered that this function of awareness and choice is called the *observer state*. This observer is the true Self, the "I," the *me* in me that is experiencing the whole drama of life.

It is this ability of being able to observe ourselves that allows us to make wise choices. Without the power of the observer we would be like robots, conditioned completely by the programming of our past experiences and learning.

We are not always conscious of this ability to be the observer of our experience. People most often experience this self-awareness in dreams, during trauma or near-death experiences, in meditation and other spiritual experiences, on certain mind-altering drugs, and when they choose to quiet their minds and reflect. However, we can *choose* to live our lives with more awareness of the observer state and thus increase our capacity to make wise decisions and choices. It is only when we make this choice to be aware that we are free from the constraints of the ego self. We begin to live our lives from the freedom of the true Self, without the bondage of fear.

This insight about the nature of awareness and decision making being outside of the realm of the brain and habitual thought also helped me understand why the usual cognitive practices, such as cognitive reconditioning, positive thinking, and affirmations, have only short-term effects on people's lives. All of these practices are in the domain of the ego self and not in the domain of the true Self. Thus they are incapable of increasing their level of consciousness; instead they can only rearrange conditioned thinking. Change occurs on a horizontal level, that is, individuals move from negative habits of thought to more positive patterns, but their awareness of themselves as "the thinker" is not increased.

With a change in the level of consciousness, a person has more awareness of when he or she is caught up in habitual thinking that is self-destructive. They are also aware of choices that were invisible to them at a lower level of awareness. A change in level of consciousness is analogous to climbing a mountain. At lower levels the climber can only see the trees that they are walking through on their way to the mountain. As they gain altitude, they see that, in fact, they were in a large forest. As they climb higher, they realize that beyond the forest is a city, a lake and a river. Still higher, they see that the mountain they are climbing is part of an entire mountain range. As they go up, they must adjust to the change in oxygen and acclimate as one does in a change in level of consciousness. It may even feel disorienting from time to time. As they climb still higher, they see that beyond the mountain range is the horizon and that we are all part of something much larger—a round planet. In the same way, as our level of consciousness rises, we eventually see that we are much larger than we imagined and are connected to our Divine nature—that we are spiritual Beings.

Choosing from the Unlimited Self

If asked, most of us would say and believe that we are free to choose. However, when we choose from the ego self of conditioned thought, we are limited to what we know, what is in memory. For example, if a person is unhappy with their job, if their level of consciousness doesn't change, they might quit but then choose a similar job situation, though it would initially appear totally different. Because the person's way of thinking hadn't changed, they would likely fall into the same undesirable job experience over time. The same would be true of changing relationships. If the level of how we perceive reality and interpret the circumstances remains constant, the horizontal level of change will be temporary. At best, our circumstances would improve, but not our level of happiness or peace of mind.

If, however, a person makes a vertical shift in their level of consciousness, he or she sees a whole new world and with it a whole new set of options. As we live more from the true Self, we see more and more possibilities.

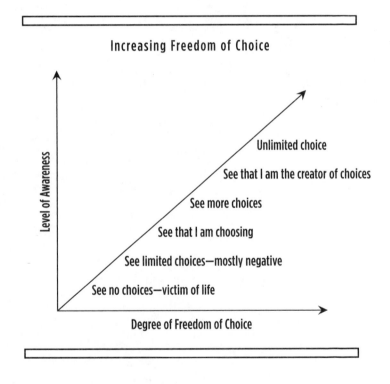

Increasing Freedom of Choice

Level of Awareness

Unlimited choice
See that I am the creator of choices
See more choices
See that I am choosing
See limited choices—mostly negative
See no choices—victim of life

Degree of Freedom of Choice

A friend of ours talked to us recently about the change in his life over the past two years. He was extremely open to what we shared with him about the principles in this book. When we met him, he had become bored with his career and was looking for something new to do. His mind was extremely busy, and though he was a hard worker, he never seemed to get anywhere in life with his relationships or his business. Once he changed his state of mind (level of consciousness), he saw a whole new way to run his business. He moved his offices, found a new clientele, changed his way of teaching his programs, and has now opened several new schools and trained a group of people to do what he had been doing by himself. He is filled with creativity, and his business is more successful than he ever imagined. Unable to write a year ago, he is now about to publish his first book. He lives in a feeling of awe and perpetual gratitude. He is working smarter, not harder, and has time to reflect, grow, and discover new and better ways to live and do his work.

When we make choices consciously, with full awareness, we are better able to see the unlimited potential of the true Self. We are free of the constraints of self-imposed beliefs about what is possible, likely, deserving, and conceivable.

The following story was written by a former student of mine who, through the power of choice, overcame her fear of a life-threatening illness that most of us dread—cancer. Her story illustrates how an awareness of the power of choice and thought can help us overcome our own addiction to fear.

Cancer Doesn't Scare Me Anymore

Cancer is a word often spoken in hushed, doom-filled tones. We feel fear in our hearts when we hear the word. Who gives us that fear? We do it to ourselves.

The first time the fear of cancer flooded my thoughts was when I was twelve years old. I was writing a health report about cells multiplying out of control; it was called cancer. I sat at my desk terrified that one day it would invade my body. Later, when I was nineteen, I witnessed my dear uncle crying his heart out as he described his beautiful wife dying of this dreaded disease. In between and since, I have listened to family members talking in those hushed tones about so and so who was battling cancer. Every time my emotions filled with fear.

In September 1998, I was told I had cancer. I was terrified. Should I clean out my drawers and make out my will? Over the course of chemotherapy, radiation, corrective and many exploratory surgeries, I observed that cancer wasn't scaring me; I was.

It's very simple. We scare ourselves with our thoughts. Now, when cancer enters a conversation, I observe my thoughts. When my thoughts picture that black, hairy devil lurking in my body, I dismiss them.

When I was first diagnosed with cancer, I felt betrayed by my body, helpless, and out of control. My days became filled with doctor appointments, crowded waiting rooms, huge humming machines peering into my body, treatments, needles, and most of all, fear. And, oh yes, that dreaded look on the face of my well-meaning family and friends as they talked about my "battle." They thought my battle was with cancer. It wasn't; it was with my thoughts.

I am forever grateful to my loving husband, family, friends, doctors, and nurses for their attention and support as I made the journey through diagnosis and treatments. One of my special memories is when a business colleague and his son, who were away on a hunting trip, called me from a duck blind in Canada to encourage me with the words, "Never give up, never give up."

I believe it was during that phone call that I *decided* (*the point of choice*) to practice what I had been taught. For twenty years my avocation had been studying the power of the mind. I had read hundreds of books and attended countless lectures, seminars, and workshops, but it took cancer to teach me what I had to learn.

The human mind is powerful. It can be used to our detriment or for our benefit. For good or evil. I decided to give up what was making me miserable, my fear. I was scaring myself to death. It was up to me.

Following that realization, my moments became peaceful, almost serene. Maybe it was the wonder drugs my doctor was giving me to relax. (My husband and I frequently called my oncologist "Mr. Chemical Man" because he had a drug for everything.) But it wasn't the drugs. It was me. I was deciding what thoughts I was going to pay attention to (*and empower with choice*). I became aware of how fear had invaded my life more than the cancer. And to be honest, fear was deteriorating my quality of life more than the cancer.

What a relief. My mind quieted down, and peacefulness surrounded me. (*Fear is very noisy.*) As my mind quieted I became aware of my life beyond cancer. Suddenly, the doctor appointments had moments of comedy, and I spent my chemo treatments getting to know my wonderful chemo nurse, Marty, and my fellow chemo patients. I'll never forget the day when my husband, a fellow patient, and I were having a great time laughing about something or other during one of my treatments. Marty turned around with his hand on his hip and a stern look on his face and said, "You people are having entirely too much fun in here." We laughed some more. When living with fear, cancer has no sense of humor. Letting go of the heavy thoughts of fear allows room for light thoughts, and joy enters in.

My new life with cancer continued. I had challenges to meet. Such as the day my doctor told me the spot on my lung was waking him up at night and we had to find out what it was; my world turned black again. Fear returned. I held onto it for about two hours. Yes, it was two hours too many, but again I observed how I was scaring myself. It wasn't the cancer; it was my thoughts. I quieted my mind. I let go of the noisy thoughts. The next time I talked to my doctor I heard his words of wisdom clearly. "Things have a way of working out," he said. Had I still been in that dark noisy world of fear, I would not have heard him. Since I was still undergoing radiation treatments, I had many days and weeks to wait for the diagnostic exploratory lung surgery. During those days of waiting, I treasured the quiet thought: *Things have a way of working out.*

It is interesting how fear lurks in the corners of the best moments. After lung surgery I was sitting in my house one day, and I started counting the bouquets of flowers that were everywhere—forty-six, to be exact. Did I think, *Oh, how wonderful to have so many thoughtful friends and family?* No, I started to ask my husband for the pathology report, because I was certain he was keeping from me the dread news that they had found cancer, even though the doctor told me they hadn't. But I stopped and observed how fear was back and ruining a special moment. I reminded myself of what was really happening. I was scaring myself. Oh, what we do to ourselves to make our lives miserable.

Now you might be thinking, they didn't find cancer, so she doesn't have to live in fear. No, they didn't find cancer, but they found a disease that killed my mother. Have I ever had a fearful thought about that disease? No. Go figure. Which again shows me that if we are afraid, it is because we are doing it to ourselves with our thoughts. The good news is that we are in control of our thoughts. We think what we *choose* to think.

I changed my fear about cancer when I saw a billboard that said, "Cancer doesn't scare me anymore." The change happened in a moment after decades of fearing cancer. To this day, I don't know if I really saw that billboard, or if the thought just came to my mind. It really doesn't matter. I gave up. I gave up fearful cancer thoughts.

Life is good, but I know that if someday my doctor says my number is up, I know I will be taken care of and I am not afraid. As my wise doctor said, "Things have a way of working out." *Cancer doesn't scare me anymore.*

REMINDERS

1. We create our world through the power of choice.
2. Choice is using the power of the mind to create something out of nothing.
3. We are always choosing and creating our lives—either through the limited, memory-bound ego self or the limitless, creative true Self.
4. Our feelings, which are either based on fear or love, function as guidance to make us aware of the source of our decisions.
5. The observer state allows us to be aware of the quality of what we are choosing and creating.
6. Our freedom to choose and create increases exponentially as our awareness level grows.
7. Choice is the power we have as human beings to create fear-proof lives.

CHAPTER 6
Listening Within
THE KEY TO KNOWING ONE'S SELF

How can we know which of our thoughts and responses come from our true voice? How can we best uncover our true Self? We do this by discovering the power of *listening within*. We all have the sensory experience of listening—to the sound of a bird singing, the voice of a loved one, the television or radio, the warning sounds of a fire engine. Deep listening, or listening within, is different than sensory listening. It is listening with the heart rather than the ear. It is listening for the invisible messages that come from others, the environment, or from our true Self. It is only when the busy mind is "on hold" and out of the jurisdiction of the ego thought system that the heart can listen.

This state of deep listening is available when our mind is calm, quiet, and reflective. A quiet mind is not dull and incapable of action, as some might assume upon hearing the words *calm* or *quiet*. It is intrinsically charged with the potentiality of action, much like the meditative awareness that a cat naturally employs before it releases its coiled energy and springs forth with precision accuracy. The stillness contained within the state of deep listening is pure awareness.

When we are listening with the ego, we tend to hear only with our ears and interpret and filter what we hear through our thought system. Our thought system is more of a *projector* than a receiver. It hears only what it wants and expects to hear. It hears only what is in agreement with its previous beliefs about life.

In order to access the wisdom contained within our soul, we must learn to listen in a new way, a way that transcends the limitations of the brain and the intellectual mind. We must discover how to access the voice of the heart—Universal Intelligence.

Yesterday I was on the way to my cabin. It is winter and I thought about stopping along the way and going cross-country skiing. Although it was a beautiful day and I had plenty of time, something inside told me to not to stop. I listened to that still inner voice because I *know* to trust it. Lucky for me that I did, because when I arrived at the parking lot where I store my car and trailer while I am at the cabin (my cabin is a ten-mile ride to an island over the ice on a snowmobile), I discovered that it was not plowed and I got stuck. It took a neighbor and me an hour to dig out the car and trailer, leaving me just enough time to get to the cabin before dark. If I had gone skiing I would have had a much more difficult time. Listening within can warn us of unforeseen danger and make our lives safer and more comfortable and thus can break our addiction to fear.

In this chapter we explore how we can come to know the true Self that is the core of who we are. We will learn how we can access the inner wisdom that will guide us to live safe and fearless lives. We will see how we can come to accept that *the voice within is our true voice, because the true Self is who we are.* We do this by discovering the power of *listening within.*

The Power of Reflection to Transform Our Lives

It is necessary to look into a full-length mirror to see a full image of ourselves. Through the magic of a mirror, a complete picture of our physical presence immediately appears. The psychological and spiritual process of reflection works in as simple a manner. The mirror we use is the process of asking ourselves honest questions.

As you engage in the process of reflection, make the conscious choice; that is, make the conscious requirement that your answers come directly from your true Self rather than from the ego thought system. In other words, *ask for your Divine perspective. Then listen quietly for the answers.* This amazingly simple practice requires a small amount of understanding of the process—and a large amount of *willingness* to ask the questions and then listen respectfully to your true Self for the answers.

Trusting Ourselves

Most of us have been taught not to trust ourselves. Many of us have learned to trust the opinions of others over our own insightful answers. Unconsciously we have relied on our intellect and ego-based belief system to find the answers. For most of us, however, this misplaced trust has proven fully unsatisfactory. Indeed, it has often led to our confusion, self-doubt, and ambivalence about a decision or response to a challenging situation. For others it has led to a self-righteous surety that is rigid and limited by set opinions and beliefs, interspersed with feelings of unacknowledged self-doubt.

In spite of our mistrust of the voice of our inner Self, that quiet voice of truth persistently comes to us. We are temporarily able to hear and distinguish its validity in moments of despair, in times of great need, and when our psychological defenses are down. This inadvertent openness to the voice of the true Self can occur when we are coming out of a deep sleep, when we experience moments of profound beauty, or in moments of crisis—all times when the intellect stops momentarily.

One such time when our collective thought system stopped and we opened ourselves to the true Self within was directly after the 9/11 attacks. The profound level of love, generosity, unity of purpose, and true compassion shared by Americans offered great hope for humanity and gave me great hope in my own life. I happened to be in New York City shortly after that tragedy, and I was overwhelmed by how helpful and friendly New Yorkers were with one another—and with me. The nature of that crisis seemed to bring out the best in all of us. Rudolph Giuliani, the mayor of New York at the time, rose to the occasion to inspire and unite the people not only of that city, but of the entire country. He provided all of us with a vision of how the world can be in a time of crisis—and even of fear. Volunteers, money, and letters of support poured into New York from around the world as a symbol of a united spirit and as an expression of our love for one another. This was an expression of our true Selves at work in the face of a great tragedy.

This inner voice, and the Universal Intelligence it represents, is with us always, even during more ordinary events. Many of us remember, thinking back on a difficult decision or events in our lives, that *something inside me* knew *that was going to happen; or I knew what I should have done, but I ignored my own conscience and common sense and did what I was told to do, or believed I should do, out of insecurity*. This inner knowing that is familiar to all of us is the voice of our true Self trying its hardest to get our attention. When we trust it and listen to its wisdom, our life is easier, more harmonious, and is truthful. We are joyful when we listen to and trust the voice of our true Self. The voice of truth is ever-present in us, though we rarely tune in to what it has to offer because our minds are too busy or are filled with fear.

Sadly, so many of us have such little trust in that voice that it has become obscure to us—unheard and unseen. We have not been consciously aware that it is the voice of our Divinity in which we can confidently place our trust. We confuse the voice of our true Self with the ramblings of our memories, belief systems, and even our own intellect (and that of others). We question what is real. Even when we begin to develop a relationship with our Self, we continue to wonder, *Is this really true, or is it my ego-based self-centeredness fooling me again?* In order to understand what is indeed "real," we need to explore the power and process of reflection in our lives.

The Source of Wise Reflection

Reflection can come to us in a silent thought like a voice in our head. It can also come to us while we are having a conversation. It can be pure thought that comes to us while in the shower or on a walk, or while writing in a journal or in quick scribbles on a convenient piece of paper. It can come to us in a song lyric that we know is expressing an inner truth. It often comes in hearing the wisdom of a child. Truth is truth; but whether it enters our awareness from inside of us or from an external source, it is always our true Self that recognizes it as truth.

A flash of insight is instantaneous. More happens in that powerful little moment than we are usually aware of. If we could view an insight in slow motion, we would notice that the initial impact of the insight comes in the form of a pure *experience* that is void of description. After that, we have thoughts or words we use to try to express what we experienced. You know this on some level but have rarely taken a meditative moment to notice the sequence.

It's much like tasting an exotic fruit you've never before tried. The first bite is a pure abstract experience that is impossible to adequately describe, though quickly (from societal training) we categorize our experiences by defining them with explanations of good, bad, or comparisons to previous experiences.

In the case of a true spiritual insight, the words may come quickly and may be as accurate as words could hope to be, since our Spirit inspired them; but they are just touchstones that remind us of our true experience. Remember as with the sampling of the exotic fruit (or your first contact with anything new), the experience itself was all that was real; the description would be nothing without the initial experience. That would be like someone describing the exotic fruit without ever seeing or tasting it.

In the case of reflective insight, the *experience* we're having is a direct experience of our Spirit (but we don't recognize that because we are unfamiliar with who we truly are). This experience of our true Self (not the words or thoughts about it) is the true catalyst that changes our level of consciousness. I believe it is important to make this distinction early on so that one does not become invested in what may seem to be a particular process (writing, walking, and so on) and miss the source.

If we're not careful to remain in our Divine reflective state at the moment of our experience, we will put ourselves back into the box of our belief system and lose the Divine Intelligence of the experience. The unnoticed pattern of opting for information from our ego thought system rather than from our Divine Intelligence permeates our lives most of the time and stunts our progress. That is why spiritual progress is relatively slow and sometimes appears to be nonexistent. However, the more we choose to wake up and listen deeply to our inner intelligence, the more our lives will benefit from and show the results.

Somehow we are socialized to see people who live reflective lives as lazy, unproductive, and less valuable than the workaholic heroes of our business and professional worlds. We are forced to ask ourselves why we ought to give up the "busyness" that has seemingly made us so great in order to take valuable time to reflect on our selves and our lives.

The reality is that when we take the time to reflect, we live our lives more *consciously*. We are no longer running around like chickens with our heads cut off, but instead we are living our lives with intention and purpose. We quit doing what is not important, that which is not inspired by or based on truth. We discover ways of doing things that are ethical, moral, and in alignment with our conscience. In other words, our actions in the world finally match our heartfelt desires, values, and instincts. We live life *wholeheartedly* when we reflect on the direction we are going. Without taking time for reflection, we react from habit-bound practices that are irrelevant, inefficient, and stressful. It is no wonder that our business and government leaders are so caught up in the many scandals of corruption and loss of ethical standards, when they are so often driven by the ego—greed, lust for power, and an insatiable need to be admired and liked.

In order to break our addiction to fear, we need to be willing to let go of the familiarity of our habitual thinking and the false sense of security it promises but never delivers.

The Adventure of Living in the Unknown

Living a life from reflection is like going on an adventure to an unknown land. We have to stop and become oriented from time to time. We need to look at a map and consult our compass, stop and observe our surroundings and landmarks, so that we know where we are and where we are going. A life without reflection is like striking out into an unknown land and spending great amounts of energy getting lost—yet ending up back where you started, having unknowingly and unwittingly walked in a circle.

Many of our social institutions operate without reflection; they continue to do things "the way they've always been done." Their lack of creativity and reflection is costing them success, relevance, and the ability to evolve and transform. The same is true in our personal lives. When we live our lives from reflection, we can access the very source of change, creativity, insight, inspiration, vision, and hope.

One Path toward Getting to Know One's Self

Written reflection is one of the many means for the voice of truth to come to us. Writing is not the best or the only way to explore and get to know your Self; your *dedication and intention* to discover your Divinity is really all that is important. The reason I emphasize the process of written reflection is that it has the added benefit of realigning us to our true Self and helping us to see who we really are—Divine Beings. When we hear the wisdom that lies just beneath the surface, we are awestruck with the power and knowledge we possess. What we see reflected in the act of writing, and in later reading what we have written, provides a powerful, self-correcting mechanism that is otherwise elusive in our fast-paced, "get-it-done-now" lifestyle.

The Benefits of Written Reflection

One example of the benefits of written reflection comes vividly to mind. It is the story of one woman's experience during a seminar of mine, but her experience parallels that of many people who engage in written reflection for the first time. During this seminar I had, as usual, sent everyone off to the gardens of our retreat space to reflect. The woman in question returned very disappointed in her attempt. She listened in awe as each participant read aloud what had come to him or her in the garden.

When it came to her turn, she sheepishly announced that she didn't really have anything worth reading. I asked her if she would read it anyway. As she read, a calm and inner knowing came over the group. What she thought was worthless was powerfully affecting the group. When she finished, she looked up with a new light in her face, which revealed that she just "heard" what she had written. Many members then responded, saying that although her question may have been personal to her, the answer profoundly applied to them as well. This is just one of the many examples of the benefits of writing and rereading reflections.

As I mentioned earlier, written reflection is only one way to reflect and access the voice of our true Self. However, it has many benefits that are not always apparent in other methods of reflection:

- When we reread what we have written, the words reflect back to us the power and truthfulness of the wisdom that is in each of us.
- When we "hear" what we have written, it reinforces that our true Self is completely reliable, honest, loving, and on our side.
- We begin to realize that the voice we hear in our reflections is the real us, and the habits of the ego and the intellectual belief system we have constructed are illusionary creations.
- We begin to trust ourselves more and act on the wise advice we hear.

Written reflection is like hearing the clear voice of our conscience.

When we know the truth of our Being, we are capable of displaying enormous amounts of courage in our daily lives because we are being guided from within in each of the opportunities and challenges that face us each day. Aligning with our true Self is uniting with the power of Universal Intelligence. With this power comes a knowing and a confidence that cannot be propelled by the ego.

Engaging in the Process of Reflection

So how do you begin this process of getting to know the true Self? The following are guidelines to use when engaging in the process of reflection.

Willingness

The first and most important stage of the process is to approach listening to your true Self with an attitude of willingness. I think of willingness as an open mind free of prejudice, without any expectation of any particular outcome or answer, and an attitude of openness to consider whatever comes, even if it doesn't happen to coincide with what you might think you normally believe (which is often the case).

This kind of willingness gives the true Self an opening to be heard. It is like the silence in a conversation that allows the other person to speak.

Pride and Not Knowing

The opposite of willingness is pride. Pride expresses itself in such statements as *By now I should know something as obvious as that,* or *I'm not an idiot, you know!* Pride, of course, stems from the ego, that false part of us that thinks we always know how to act, what to do, and what the answer is. Pride keeps us in the illusionary safety of what we think we already know. Thus, pride keeps us from leaping into the *unknown*—where, in fact, new answers uncontaminated by the ego thought system await discovery.

When we turn from pride to willingness, we begin to accept that there are things in our lives, and life in general, that we do not know. Nature itself is not bound by definite outcomes. It is creation unfolding; it is a work in progress of endless possibilities, and so it is with our lives as well.

When we begin to experience willingness and trust in our true Selves, we become comfortable with being in a state of "not knowing." We see this state as natural and nothing to be afraid of. We understand that the unknown is not scary; rather it is an invitation to discover more of who we truly are.

What is unknown to us on a conscious level is easily known by our Spirit, and that is comforting. We realize that not only can our questions be answered, but they also have a purpose. The purpose is to ask our Self, and in the asking and the listening, we bring more of our Spirit into our conscious awareness. The unknown is nothing more than our true Selves unrevealed; and to reveal this true state of consciousness brings us all the answers we need to have to live life as it is intended.

Discovery

A sense of discovery has led explorers to new lands and planets, it has led scientists to find cures and inventions that enrich and extend our lives. It is a sense of discovery that enables spiritual leaders to discover the source of truth—and to discover that truth within. Curiosity and discovery pull us forward toward the unknown, make us take the turn around the next corner, up and over the next mountain range, and into the sources of our insight and of our very mysteries. The great mysteries of life reveal themselves as we fend our way with curiosity along the uncertain path, wondering and questioning our way through the darkness.

Discovery and what we think of as the unknown are inextricably linked. Curiosity leads to questions and, as we mentioned earlier, questions enable us to discover the truth of who we are. For example, I begin each day either sitting quietly or writing in my journal and asking my Self if I have anything to say today. I ask myself:

- What is my purpose for this day?
- Is there anything I need to focus my attention on?
- Is there a problem or issue I need to address?
- Is there something I am inspired to do—write, call a friend, clean my office, something else?

Being open and asking questions leads me to discover an interesting and purpose-filled life.

Asking Questions

When we ask a question, it is as though we pick up the phone to our true Self and dial the number. First, we wait for a dial tone—we ask ourselves if we are really willing. Next, we ask the question. Then, we listen.

If we don't get an answer right away, we might want to ask ourselves:

- Am I asking the right question?
- Might there be a better way to ask this question?
- Is it the right time to ask this question?

You will be amazed at the responses you hear.

The questions themselves derive from the curiosity that comes from an attitude of discovery. After all, it takes a certain amount of innocence to ask a question. That's why children ask questions all the time. And we are always innocent if we are truly honest with ourselves. We don't know the next step in life, we only think we do. It is innocence that will allow us to hear from beyond the knowledge of our limited, ego belief system. Yet innocence takes humility as well. You can't ask a sincere question without acknowledging that you don't know. Accepting that you don't know creates the opening for a question to occur to you.

For example, a year and a half ago I injured my back. I was in great pain and flat on my back for more than a week. In my reflections I asked what to do for my pain and injury. At every juncture, I asked my Self for guidance in the healing and recovery process. Each time I was given the perfect prescription for realizing my health. I felt guided to just the right doctors, acupuncturist, healers, and physical rehabilitation. I healed very quickly and am now in better shape than I can remember being in before my injury.

Letting Go of Expectations and Preconceptions

What blocks our hearing a truthful answer is often the simple fact that we have a preconceived notion of what the answer is going to be. We all generally have a preconceived idea of the answer, but that doesn't mean we have to put any stock in it. Choosing to give up our preconceived notions is an example of willingness and humility—of realizing that we may be wrong, or simply haven't a clue to the answer. It is only when we can let go of expectations of what we are going to hear that we let down the defenses that keep us from listening deeply.

Listening deeply is listening with nothing on your mind but the question. Listening deeply quiets the mind, so that the mind can hear the answer. By being open rather than searching your intellect for the answer, your memories and beliefs do not limit you. In my healing of my back, this openness led me to seek out solutions that were out of my conscious awareness. For example, it occurred to me during a written reflection to contact an old friend whom I hadn't seen in years about taking a class in Qi Gong. He, in turn, connected me with a personal weight trainer who helped me transform my back injury.

A Quiet Mind

Another important part of the process of reflection is having a quiet mind. In the midst of our modern-day society of stretched-to-the-limit schedules, multi-tasking, stress, and little free time, we seldom find ourselves enjoying a quiet mind. Yet without a quiet mind, how can we even find the place where the door to reflection and the true Self exists? When the mind is preoccupied or busy, it is like getting a busy signal when we want to call our true Self. We can't connect, because the circuits are already tied up with our own thoughts.

My mother used to say, "An idle mind is the devil's workshop." This adage assumes that when the mind is quiet, it somehow leaves room for the "devil" to come in and do the devil's work. It makes the assumption that we are separate from God. Not only separate from God, but that we are evil, sinners, lazy, and no good.

Nothing is further from the truth. We are *all* born good, holy, and complete. It is only when we fail to trust ourselves that we create the separation between God and ourselves. Knowing that we are at one with the Divine allows us to relax our guard. We can quiet our minds and embrace the spiritual wisdom that is within each of us. I prefer to replace my mom's adage with "A quiet mind is God's workshop." It is only when our mind is quiet that we can hear the voice of God, the voice of our true Self.

Acceptance

Often when I do a written reflection, my mind will begin by wandering all over the map until I finally settle down into a quiet mind. I know that I can't get from a busy mind to a quiet mind by trying to control myself or by judging my busy mind. The only way through this maze of thought is through *complete* self-acceptance. Ironically, only when I finally accept my busy, distracted mind can I move in the direction of quiet.

Everyone may approach letting go of his or her busy thinking differently. It's not about techniques but rather what might occur to you in the form of inspiration that is appropriate for that moment. Sometimes just noticing that you're caught up in your thinking can lead to a quiet mind. Other times you may distract yourself by moving on to other things. What's most important is to know that it's possible to have a peaceful mind, and just as important, if you aren't experiencing peace, to accept where you are at the time.

Letting It Flow

Now that you are willing, you've let go of expectations, you're open to discovery, your mind is quiet, and you are listening deeply, how does the voice of your true Self actually begin to speak?

The fact is that sometimes there is a long silence. Other times your insecure thinking and distracted, busy mind takes over again. But if you are trusting, accepting, and patient, that voice does begin to speak. Don't judge what comes or second-guess what it means. Sometimes at first it is a quiet, tentative voice, but soon it comes more quickly.

For me it comes first as a feeling (an experience) that has no words. It is like seeing a picture of an answer in my imagination, or having a gut feeling that doesn't yet have words of expression, but that I can *feel* coming. I know before I can explain, with words, how I know.

It is important to not force the words. The words will come in time. An insight must be birthed—first it is conceived, then it gestates and grows, and only after the answer is ready does it birth in the form of a language of words. When I express a written reflection, I usually have no idea what word will follow the one before it. I just let it flow and trust that it will make sense when I am done. I don't even look at the words as I place them on the page or in my mind. I don't try to anticipate where the words are going, nor do I anticipate when the flow of words will stop. I don't judge what is coming even if it sounds nonsensical. I often feel like I am losing all control and that something is taking over. Something *is* taking over, and it is my—and our—true Self. Once we get our inner critic, our doubter, and our judge out of the way, our reflections begin to flow.

When the flow of insight and inspiration comes, it is a joyous and energizing experience. I am often in awe of what comes out of my pen or my computer. *Did I really say that?* The voice of the true Self can sound unfamiliar in the beginning because we are so used to the ramblings of our limited and arrogant ego and memory. In the beginning it is like getting to know a new friend. You may feel awkward, untrusting, and even a little defensive. Over time you will discover that your true Self is a best friend to whom you can tell anything and who will never judge you. It will only love, accept, and help you. This doesn't mean the voice of the true Self is weak or a wimp, unwilling to engage or even challenge you. My own inner voice often challenges and confronts my limited thinking. The voice of the true Self speaks with resolve, authority, and a knowing that cannot be challenged.

For a while I was meeting with a group of friends that were practicing the process I have just described. We would often read excerpts from our reflections to one another. One of the striking observations we all had is that the answers each of us received, though they seemed to apply to a particular and very personal question, always applied universally to everyone in the group. Later as I brought this process to others in my seminars, the same was true. This universal application is the very nature of truth. When one reads truth, it seems as relevant now as it did two thousand years ago or will two thousand years from now. Truth is timeless, universal, and yet at the same time personal and existing in what we perceive as our own time.

Written reflection becomes easier and more natural over time. Like anything you practice, the more you do it, the more effective you are. There may be days when there is nothing you want to say or ask. Don't judge yourself if you miss a day or even many days. Each time you return to the process, your true Self will welcome you back. When you have a relationship with your Divine nature, you find yourself becoming more your Self each day. In fact, as time goes on you will begin to receive answers to questions without having to sit down and write them out. As one of my seminar participants recently said:

I love the wisdom of the written reflections but I don't do it very often. However, I do tend to have little thoughts or ideas that help a situation if I just stop and allow myself a quick regrouping. This may be for only 10–15 seconds to pause in the middle of a business meeting. It has proven very helpful to move through an impasse in a negotiation that is very sensitive. It is amazing, the truth that comes from within. I apply this same on-the-go reflection to fear when it comes up. I just stop and ask myself what the fear is alerting me to, and I get the information I need to move on and regain my bearings.

For others, written reflection is a daily practice that begins or ends their day. There are no rules or formulas for what works. Each of us is unique. The important thing is to take time to listen within for the guidance that is always available to each of us.

Blocks to Listening to Our Inner Voice

Before I leave this discussion of written reflection, I would like to summarize some of the common obstacles that can get in the way of listening to this important inner resource.

I'm Too Busy

It is easy to stay swept up in the fast pace of our lives and choose not to take the time to listen for our true Selves. If we don't choose to make a relationship with the true Self a priority in our lives, it will never happen. Being willing, curious, and trusting our ability to listen will inspire us to do what it takes.

If we decide to make a relationship with the true Self a priority, we may find that we need a more formalized approach to overriding the habitual busy state of our minds. It wasn't until I consciously set aside real time for reflection that I started to stay in that Divine space throughout the day.

When we take the time to reflect and develop this primary relationship with our true Self, everything else in our lives will fall into place more easily. The true Self is the anchor that will keep us safe, the balance that will allow us to enjoy our lives, and the calm that will bring a deep sense of peace.

It's Too Scary

Entering into the unknown of your true Self takes courage, more courage than anything you will ever do in your life. Entering the unknown is like walking into the darkness. Yet only your imaginings of what lurks in the darkness frighten you. What always surprises people who do make the choice to enter the unknown of the true Self is that, ultimately, everything they hear and realize is always loving, benevolent, and encouraging. Your true Self will never judge you, reject you, or hurt you. Once you shine the light of awareness on the unknown, you will see that there is only help and guidance. There is only the love that leads you back home to your true Self. After a while you will be so curious to see what is around the next corner of your life that you will find yourself seeking out the unknown, rather than fearing it.

We Don't Trust Ourselves

Who, me? How could I trust advice or counsel that comes from me? This deep mistrust of our own Self comes from seeing ourselves as separate from God. When we see ourselves as this little ego self, all alone in this frightening, threatening world, we become the last person to turn to for the source of truth and guidance. Much of my life I looked to those whom I perceived as wiser, more knowledgeable, and more deserving of respect than myself. I looked for them in books, teachers, counselors, and spiritual advisors—and they all had many wonderful and helpful things to say to me. Ultimately, however, I knew had to trust myself. The truth is that I am the only one who knows how to live my life. I am not alone and I am not separate from every other being, but I am the only one who is responsible for my own life. I am the only one who can direct my life, make my decisions, and choose my path. I know that I can navigate that path by listening to and trusting in my own common sense and wisdom. If I can't trust myself, who can I trust?

I Am Unworthy

I don't deserve to live a happy life. I haven't suffered enough, or grown enough, or learned enough. This is perhaps the most common barrier to listening to the true Self I have heard from those who begin down this path of Self-discovery. When they consciously realize that the only person or circumstance keeping them from living a life of heaven on earth is himself or herself, they come up with a hundred reasons why they can't have what they've always wanted. Whatever the reason, it always boils down to *I'm not worthy.*

We are all worthy. There are no exceptions. We are all born to realize and live as our Divine Selves. The judgment day is here, and *you* are the judge. Will you let yourself into the kingdom of heaven? Remember: The kingdom of heaven is within.

Maybe I'll Hear Something I Don't Want to Hear

What if I don't like the answer I get, or what if it's wrong, or what if I will have to change the way I do things? What if I'm told to change my career, my marriage, where I am living, the way I eat, drink, or smoke? This is a very common obstacle to taking the time to reflect. People will spend years running from the truth of being in the wrong job, the wrong relationship, not fulfilling their purpose in life. Why? Because they might have to change, and they see change as a threat to the equilibrium of their lives. *But this is the way I have always coped. I don't know if I would be successful at that. At least I know I can do this. Or, that might mess up my life plan. I thought I knew where I was going in life.*

When we do things out of habit, we lose our power to create and choose our lives—the definition of freedom. We become prisoners of our own thoughts, beliefs, and limitations. This fear of change sits in the very heart of the ego. The ego wants to do what it perceives as safe, normal, sane, acceptable, and as the way it has always been done. Our true Self cries to us in a whisper—listen to me, trust me, all will be well if you do.

When we ask a real question, we will never get an answer that would ever do harm to us in any way. The answer will only make our lives easier, healthier, more meaningful, happier, and more purposeful. We can discover this truth only if we make the leap of faith and have the courage to listen within to our Selves and follow our own Divine advice.

All of these obstacles are aspects of the face of fear. *Fear is the only thing that can keep us from our Selves.* I've even known people who choose to ignore their own wise reflections. At first it was almost inconceivable to me that one could bring forth so much Divine truth and then ignore it. I was reminded, from their example, that choice is a constant, free-will creative power that we can use or abuse at any time. We can choose fear or our Divinity, from moment to moment.

Fear is just an illusion of thought that we create to keep us from knowing our true Selves. Listening within through reflection is the key that can unlock the door to the freedom we have all dreamed of. We can recover from our addiction to fear.

REMINDERS

1. Reflection has the following benefits for us:
   - We live a wholehearted life, congruent with our values, purpose, and truth.
   - We live our lives from a feeling of confidence, resolve, and certainty, instead of from confusion and ambivalence.
   - We are aligned with our true purpose in life rather than aimlessly living from mere force of habit.
   - We make decisions that are courageous, true, aligned with our heart, and inspiring to others.
   - We handle practical decisions for business, finances, health, diet, and relationships with more ease and wisdom.
   - Our lives become interesting, expansive, and an adventure that is never boring.
   - We live our lives driven by love rather than by fear.
2. The process of quiet reflection reveals our true Selves.
3. Willingness and an acknowledgment that we don't know all the answers provide an opening for the true Self to speak.
4. An attitude of discovery leads to curiosity and questions—the key to uncovering the unknown.
5. Honest questions lead to the humility needed for deep listening.
6. Let go of all preconceived ideas and expectations of what you will hear.
7. A quiet mind is God's workshop.
8. Acceptance without judgment transforms unwanted thoughts.
9. Insights flow when we don't try to anticipate what they will be.
10. All obstacles to listening to our true Selves are fear in its many disguises.

CHAPTER 7
Intuition
THE ANTIDOTE TO FEAR, WORRY, AND A BUSY MIND

If we have spent our entire lives thinking that fear makes us safe, helps us anticipate the future, and keeps our lives and those around us under control, then we might panic at the suggestion of letting fear go. What would replace fear if we no longer wanted to let it rule our lives?

Intuition is the antidote to fear, worry, and a busy mind. It's like a homing signal that is always there to bring us back into harmony with the peace and intelligence of our Divine nature. This inner intelligence is beyond the other senses, beyond the known information of the intellect—it is wise and connected to the whole. If we heed its guidance, we will restore our health, heal our differences, be in harmony with the planet and each other, and experience a sense of deep hope.

Intuition is the signal of information that speaks to us in the voice of Universal Intelligence, the voice of our true Self. Intuition may speak to us via a physical sensation that some call a "gut feeling." For some, this sensation manifests as a feeling in the stomach area. For others, the hair on the back of the neck stands on end. For still others, it is an overall bodily sensation. Intuition may also make itself heard in an insight, a vision, or a dream. We are uniquely encoded to hear intuition individually.

Though it is not officially recognized as one of our senses, intuition is really our sixth sense. It is the sense least developed, or may even have been lost, in many people. Due to our bias as a culture in favor of reasoning and the intellect, many people have lost all consciousness of their intuitive sense. We tend to respect only that which we can sense through the five main senses of sight, touch, hearing, smell, and taste. Our culture sees intuition as unreliable, feminine, soft, and impractical.

To add to the confusion, what many call intuitions are really just masked projections of a person's belief system or ego needs. For example, I may rationalize that I *need* a new car and that my intuition is telling me to get one, when in fact I am unhappy and am trying to fill an internal void with a material possession.

Nevertheless, all of us have the sense of intuition, and in hindsight we often reflect that "something" told us what was going to happen. Sometimes we regrettably feel we should have trusted our gut, because it was absolutely accurate.

Our Internal Radar

Intuition is an early warning system that allows us to see what is yet unknown; that is, what is invisible to the other senses. For example, quite often I will think about someone and then the phone will ring and it is that person. This is understandable with close family members, but when it is someone I haven't spoken with in years, it stands out as unusual, even a little spooky. Most of us have had this experience of intuition or know someone close to us who has, but we tend to brush if off as a coincidence. Or we reserve it for "psychic" people and feel we have no reliable access to this experience. It seems to go beyond the normal boundaries of time and space and sees into the future or what is outside the reach of the other five senses. In a sense, intuition is a way in which we are all interconnected.

If we learn to trust and rely on intuition more frequently, it has many wonderful benefits.

- *Safety:* It allows us to sense danger before it is visible.
- *Health:* It facilitates our sensing when something is off in our bodies and alerts us to see our physician, talk to a health care provider, or have testing done.
- *Balance:* It lets us know when and how much to exercise, eat, sleep, rest, and helps us plan effectively.
- *Opportunity:* It helps us sense opportunities for our career success, financial well-being, relationships, and a fun and safe life.
- *Performance:* It increases peak performance in athletics, work, creativity, and spiritual growth.
- *Calmness:* It keeps the mind calm and thus lowers stress and makes our lives more joyful because it replaces the voice of fear.

The Web of Interconnection: Intuition

Where does the information of intuition come from? Modern physics has shown us how interconnected we all are. What looks like empty space between objects is filled with many energy patterns and other invisible "things": microwaves, radio waves, microscopic organisms, subatomic particles, the digitized light and sound signals that transmit phone conversations, video images, and Internet communications, and lots that we don't yet know about. The principles of physics allow me to be at my cabin here in the Canadian wilderness and via satellite through my computer have a conversation with my wife in St. Paul, Minnesota, or a friend in Asia or Latin America. The boundaries that seem to separate us are not as real as we think, on both a physical and a mental level. We are really an interconnected web of relationships bound together in ways not apparent to us with the naked eye. These invisible connections are the runways of intuition.

Imagine yourself on an island in the middle of the ocean. Living on the island, you become accustomed to all that you see, hear, touch, smell, and taste with your senses. This island is your self-contained reality that represents all the known of your universe, all that you have learned and have stored in your intellect. However, the surface of the island is merely the part of the island that is accessible to your senses. The island goes to the bottom of the ocean and is connected to all the other islands and continents through the ocean floor. We appear separate, but only on the surface. Like all the seemingly separate islands in the ocean, we are all connected beneath the surface, and because of that interconnectedness, we are able to communicate on the intuitive level. Communication of this type is often subtle and outside of the range of our limited sensory organs.

Last summer our family business's home offices burned to the ground. Our family had a plant nursery, and our childhood home looked across the parking lot at the old nursery buildings built in the 1930s. One week before the fire, one of my family members had a prophetic dream about it. She told me about the dream in detail before the fire happened, and on the night of the fire she reminded me about it. It scared her so immensely that she could not sleep for five nights after the fire, and it was all she could think about because it was so exact—the fire stopped at the third building, just as in her dream.

How could a dream predict a future event? Most people would have dismissed this as coincidence, but intuition is a normal part of who we are. We are all connected to future possibilities and to each other through this form of Universal Intelligence.

The Power of Intuition

I am always in awe of how information flows through empty space—the satellite transmissions of phone conversations, movies, bank transactions, medical information, airplane travel route coordination, photographs, and so on. How do all those bits of information and images travel through thin air, we might wonder? We may not understand the technology, yet without any doubts that it will work, we pass money from one account to another, send confidential information over the airwaves, and trust that the planes won't end up in one anothers' flight paths.

If we can trust the invisible mysteries of technology, why can't we trust the equally invisible nature of intuition?

In the case of technology, we have faith that some scientist understands how it all works. Therefore, we don't have to figure it out for ourselves. When it comes to trusting in our own intuitive survival instincts, however, we want verifiable proof. Yet ordinary observation of our own lives and of those around us quickly shows us that when we trust this invisible power of intuition, our lives are far better off. Successful entrepreneurs, athletes, artists, scientists, musicians, and writers have all relied heavily on the many forms of intuition, including inspiration, creativity, insight, and gut instinct.

I remember reading a newspaper account of a woman who avoided a serious encounter with terrorists by trusting her intuition. She was not a psychic, but an ordinary person like you and me who happened to listen to her intuition on a particular day. She lived just outside Tokyo, Japan, and took the subway each day to work. One day she got a strong thought that she should drive her car to work that day, though she always took the subway. She questioned the thought and initially dismissed it, because parking is difficult and expensive and travel time by car is unpredictable. However, her feelings of anxiety (the form her intuition took) kept getting louder, and her inner voice told her to take the car. Finally, against reason and logic she chose to drive. That was the day terrorists planted the poison canister that led to the deaths of many people on her train. If she hadn't trusted that invisible, illogical intuitive voice, she might not be alive today.

Her intuition only appeared illogical and mysterious, but in fact it was very logical and practical.

We may not yet be able to prove the power of intuition with our present scientific instrumentation, but it is evident nevertheless. We can't see the impulses from satellites that send images to our TVs, but we still unhesitatingly turn on our sets every night. What's the difference? Trust. Trust is the result of having faith in something or someone and having it repeatedly proven to be reliable. We must take that leap of faith in our intuition in order to discover just how reliable it is.

The Myth of Vigilance in Keeping Us Safe

Intuition is like radar for sensing danger before it is present. It has all the benefits of vigilance without the negative side effects. Being mentally vigilant all the time is tiring, stressful, and keeps us from enjoying our lives. When we are mentally vigilant, our intellect, guided by our fearful belief system, attempts to create safety by compulsively thinking over and over about all the things that could go wrong in any situation. Overthinking jams the natural paths of communication between our conscious awareness and our all-knowing true Self. This obsessive habit makes us anxious, prevents us from seeing real dangers as well as all the things that are going smoothly, and thus robs us of a happy, calm life. It also creates a lot of false alarms, because our imagination, when coupled with fear, makes up all kinds of bogeymen that aren't actually there.

The beauty of intuition is that we don't have to keep our minds constantly busy thinking about all the possible things that can go amiss. Intuition is like a security system that is always on and ever vigilant, surveying not only danger, but everything else as well—when we need to change the oil, pay a bill, call a friend in need, or get the furnace serviced.

After 9/11 we heard repeatedly about the importance of being vigilant of suspicious strangers, signs of anything unusual, and a host of other fear-inducing thoughts. We were told to be especially vigilant during a code yellow or red. We weren't told exactly what to be on the lookout for, but just to maintain a general feeling of alertness. This is an impossible task and one that leads to a miserable life. It leads us to a fate of living in fear most of the time. Increased handgun and security system sales are directly the result of the level of fear in a society. So is the addiction to worry and obsession, including constant news watching, as a way to control life. Have any of these things made us safer? I would say they have made us less safe and more distant from one another, leading many of us into a numbing life of denial, withdrawal, and despair.

In my experience as a psychologist for the past thirty years, I have noticed that people who have the most fear or denial are the most likely to become victims of some calamity or misfortune. The reason for this is simple: people who are constantly fearful or in a state of denial have *perceptual blinders* on. They are so focused on their thoughts of what could go wrong that they miss the obvious dangers right in front of them. Their minds are in the future or the past but not in the present. In either case, denial or obsession, they have lost consciousness of the present moment.

When we live in the present moment, we have access to our intuition and to a clear-minded perception of reality. Being in the present moment is the only time we are able to see what is dangerous and what is not. Being aware and seeing clearly allows us to respond from wisdom to any situation that presents itself.

Animals provide a wonderful illustration of this concept. I have often noticed deer and other animals sense when a hunter is coming. I am frequently able to observe deer from close range because I am calm and pose no threat; they let me come close to them. If a hunter approaches, they scatter before I ever hear or see the hunters coming. They may have better hearing or are warned by the calls of crows, or they may just sense the hunters coming. However, the deer don't scatter when I approach because I pose no danger. How do they know that? We call it survival instinct in animals, but it is the same as intuition in humans.

One day I was walking through the park with my wife, and a dog came up to us on the path, wagging its tail and greeting us with affection. A moment later, another man came along and the same dog growled at him. The man told us he hates dogs. When we hate or fear something, we send out fermions, chemicals invisible to the naked eye but visible to a scientist with the proper instrument and to the animal that senses them. There are many things in this world that we can't see, yet they are communicating with us all the time. We need only to trust them to benefit by their messages. Intuition is the name we give to those things we can't yet see but know to trust. To be truly safe and to maintain our sense of equilibrium, we must develop a trust of and an ear for our intuition.

How Intuition Makes Us Safe

We usually think of safety in terms of seat belts, security systems, traffic laws, smoke detectors, and having a strong police and military presence. Although these precautions may make us safer, they don't give us the *feeling* of safety. There are not enough padlocks, security systems, self-defense classes, and police to make us *feel* safe, not to mention always to *be* safe. So how do we find both a feeling and an actuality of safety in our lives?

Safety is a feeling of calm, of peace of mind. When we feel safe, our minds are relaxed and, in fact, more conscious and aware. Feeling safe occurs when we let go of fear and we trust—trust in something larger than our fears. By not trusting in that something larger, we are wedded to fear and the worrisome thoughts that come with it. That something larger is what we have talked about as the true Self, our Divine connection to all the other "islands."

Some may think that if their minds were relaxed, they would be nonvigilant, off guard, and vulnerable. The opposite is true. It is only when our minds are relaxed enough that we can hear our *true* intuitive voice, which is providing us with information appropriate for each moment, information that keeps us safe. Intuition is also the gift of discernment, the ability to tell when we are in real danger or when we are making it up with a fearful state of mind.

Intuition is completely ordinary. It is not limited to psychics, women, or shamans. Although it is known by many names—gut feeling, instinct, a hunch, a knowing, an out-of-the-blue thought, our inner voice, inspiration, or a flash, *intuition is only one thing: the voice of our true Self.* When we listen to it, we are safer, happier, wiser, and experience more abundance in our lives. Intuition guides us to safety and unleashes our potential as individuals, as communities, and as a world. Intuition is what takes us into the world of unlimited possibilities.

Trusting Intuition

The more we trust our intuitive thoughts and feelings, the more conscious, clear, and prevalent they become. As I have gone through life and live it more from my true Self, the less I rely on the projections of my intellect and the more I trust in the out-of-the-blue thoughts that come into my mind from my spiritual intelligence. My intellect is now in service to the deeper intelligence of my true Self. When I don't doubt, dismiss, or hesitate in acting on these intuitive thoughts, I am always rewarded with what appears to be good luck or fortune. This is true of mundane things like finding an item I have lost, getting a deal on a purchase, or knowing to call a client or friend who is trying to reach me. It is also true in more serious matters of safety, survival, and critical life choices, like avoiding an accident, choosing a route that bypasses danger, helping a client, or meeting a potential teacher, friend, or mate.

Blocks to Intuition

How can we know if we are blocking the information of intuition? There are several major blocks:

- We have a vigilant, busy mind.
- We doubt what we sense or hear from our true Self.
- We overinterpret what we hear.
- We don't take action on the information our intuition offers.

We Have a Vigilant, Busy Mind

A mind busy with fear blocks our ability to hear, trust, and act on our intuition. Therefore, a vigilant, busy mind is a vulnerable mind. It is too preoccupied with fearful thoughts to hear the very information that can truly make us safe and sound during times of danger. It is too focused on what we expect rather than on the unexpected. A mind busy with fear has tunnel vision; it is so busy obsessing on what are often inconsequential details that it makes us less aware of our overall surroundings. When we are full of fearful thoughts, we block information that we already possess (as in test anxiety) and information that we don't yet know with our intellect but sense (when we fail to hear our intuition).

The antidote to a busy mind is not denial, but calm awareness. Calm awareness puts us in the observer state, the zone in which we are conscious, open to wise information from the true Self, and thus safe.

We Doubt What We Sense or Hear from Our True Self

Doubting the voice or guidance of our true Selves is what keeps us from everything we deserve and want in life: happiness, safety, peace of mind, self-realization. Doubting our true Selves comes from not recognizing who we are—Divine Beings in a human form. If our inspired thoughts don't coincide with our belief system, we tend to question or doubt the information that is coming. Or, we are so identified with our beliefs and ideas that we rigidly adhere to how we see life, situations, and others.

We Overinterpret What We Hear

When we are lucky enough to actually hear our intuition, we (myself included) often make the mistake of interpreting it through our preconceived belief systems, thus jumping to inaccurate conclusions about what our intuition means. Our belief systems are limited to what we have concluded in the past about ourselves, others, and life in general. Interpreting our intuition through the filter of our belief systems is like listening only to points of view that are in agreement with our own. Consequently, we only validate our existing beliefs and no new information comes in. It is better to let the information sink in than to think about it too much.

We Don't Take Action on the Information Our Intuition Offers

All of these blocks lead to inaction. Nevertheless, if you can hear your intuition and refrain from overanalysis, overinterpretation, or doubt, you may still (for whatever reason) refuse to take action. In that case the insights will be of no benefit to you.

Choosing inaction means you have chosen to continue living from the limitations of your ego belief system rather than from the boundless wisdom of your true Self. It's a path deep into denial. It is like graduating from college and not using any of the information you gained in school.

It would seem like a no-brainer to use what you know is true; why would anyone choose inaction? Because action threatens the ego's status quo. People are afraid to trust and identify with their true Selves because of their complete identification with their ego personality. And that ego personality does not deviate from what it knows. This habit is ingrained in the fabric of society. Humans, as a whole, have not made significant gains in this realization.

Our experience of our true Self is all that is truly important. So how do we know if we are sabotaging ourselves with the ego and/or kidding ourselves into believing an ego-based belief that is disguising itself as an intuition? How do we discern the difference between the voice of the Self and that of the ego?

Discerning Intuition from Projection

Intuition is pure information, uncontaminated by our personal belief systems. However, when we are afraid and off balance, we either don't hear its subtle voice or we doubt what we do hear. Sometimes our intuition is so strong that we feel a sense of certainty about it. This *knowing* that we are hearing the truth of our Self allows us to trust it. However, living with fear often triggers an intellectual response to our intuition, contaminating it with our ego-based interpretations. How do we elude the undermining effects of fear? How do we discern if what we perceive as an intuitive insight is real or imagined? This section of the chapter addresses the art of discernment and how we can hone this skill to live more fully from the wisdom of the true Self.

Intuition speaks to us no matter what our present state of mind is—be it upset, frightened, or angry. However, to hear the voice of intuition and avoid misinterpreting it, it is important to clear our heads and be still, especially during times of distress. From a state of momentary calm, even within a crisis situation, we can clearly hear the voice of wisdom. Emergency workers who deal with life-and-death situations every day know the importance of remaining calm in order to think clearly and act wisely and decisively. If they allow fear to take over, they can't think clearly and may do fatal harm to those they are enlisted to help.

It is a little-known truth that we can readily call on a calm mind and it will come to us instantly, no matter how dire our circumstances. We must summon a calm mind, for it is only when we are calm that we are able to discern the many voices and messages in our heads and know which ones are coming from fear and which are coming from the wisdom of intuition and good judgment.

Discernment

Ego Projects → Interprets (from thought system) →
Intuition → Reflects → Receives (from spiritual intelligence)

Guidelines for Discernment

In this last section of the chapter I present guidelines for discerning when the information we are receiving is true intuition or disguised ego projection. When I refer to *discernment*, I am speaking of an awareness of the quality of our thinking. To have this level of awareness, we must be in the observer state I spoke about in chapter 5. When we are in the observer state, we are operating from our true Self.

Yesterday I was speaking to my sister, whose husband has been diagnosed with a terminal disease. The doctors initially gave him five years to live, which he has already outlived. Now they give him two years at most. My sister has been afraid to allow herself to think about this possibility. She knows from experience that the doctors can be wrong, but the thought of losing her husband has been too painful and frightening to consider. When I called her yesterday, she was in the middle of taking time to reflect on this issue. Her husband is away with their sons on a fishing trip, and for the first time in a long while she is alone. Rather than fill her solitude with more activity, she decided to take this time to reflect on what life would be like without him, what she would do with her life, and how she wanted to live out the balance of her time with him, regardless of how long it may last.

As the hours went on she had a profound realization. She and her husband have always been "doers." They seem to rush from one activity and project to another, never really taking time to be quiet together and savor each other's company, though they enjoy it immensely. In a moment of clarity and reflection, she realized that they were going to change the way they lived—to slow down and take in life fully.

For my sister this realization was huge and would bring about a lifestyle change she had not considered before. She wandered around the house taking in her life, open to what might change. She went upstairs to her art studio and puttered around for a while, and she just knew that wasn't "it." Maybe at a later time, but for now other priorities were more important. As each discernment came, she let go of her fear and took the time to listen within to the source of her truth. She realized that her husband's illness really has nothing to do with this decision—it merely caused her to reflect.

How many of us never take the time to discover what is there within, trying to guide us to a better quality of life? The following are questions you can ask yourself if you want clear discernment.

- Does my feeling have a calm and balanced sense to it, or is it excited and impatient?
- Am I jumping to quick, reactive conclusions, or am I listening deeply with time for reflection?
- Are my thoughts confused, rigid, and habitual, or are they flowing, simple, and clear?
- Am I invested in the outcome, or am I open to the wisest answer—regardless if it disagrees with my past thinking, expectations, or hopes?
- Am I afraid to hear the truth and avoiding taking time for reflection, or am I courageously facing what life presents me?

Let's take each question and explore what it is pointing to.

Does my feeling have a calm and balanced sense to it, or is it excited and impatient?

As I addressed in chapter 4, "Creators of Experience," our feelings and emotions are a built-in guidance system to let us know if we are operating from the ego or the true Self. Assessing the quality of our feelings is a direct application of this concept. Early on in my discovery of these principles, I would often jump to the erroneous conclusion that my excited feelings after an apparent insight were confirmation that I was on the track of my true Self. Later, and often in humbling circumstances, I would have to admit that my ego had snuck back in and fooled me again. Over time I began to suspect the feeling of excitement, as it was often a telltale sign of ego. The excitement was about getting my way or looking good (definitely the work of the ego), not about having an intuitive glimpse from my inner Divine Intelligence.

I came to see that intuition comes with a *calm knowing* that feels balanced and truthful, but without the extra adrenaline of excitement. I am also less prone to take credit for the insight when it is true; looking good doesn't enter into the picture. Intuition has a feeling of coming from beyond me, although it is from my true Self. It may have passion and enthusiasm if it is true intuition, but neither of these feelings take me off balance; they just propel me forward.

Am I jumping to quick, reactive conclusions, or am I listening deeply with time for reflection?

Sometimes we receive intuition that we know to act on immediately. However, when we are uncertain, it is wise to take a moment or longer to reflect. The reflection can take only an instant, if the circumstances require our immediate action, as in an athletic event or a crisis. Or we can take a longer time for reflection, as in the case of written reflection that I spoke of in chapter 5. Regardless of the circumstances, it is important to check in with our true Self and then trust what we hear. If we impulsively react from habit without listening to our intuition, we often have to redo a decision later or live with the harmful consequences of it.

For example, my sister-in-law recently lost her job and called to ask if she could come up to visit my wife and me at our cabin for a week. My first reaction was to say, "Of course, we would love to have you." On a logical level it *seemed right*, but I had a slight uneasiness about it even as I said it to her. I like her and felt compassion for her losing her job, but the timing felt off. As I reflected further, it became clear that we would be trying way too hard to cram another visitor into that particular time slot. We already had someone coming to the cabin that same week and when I mentioned it to our friend, she was obviously disappointed that someone else would be joining us.

Ultimately, my sister-in-law didn't have the legal permit to come into Canada and couldn't get it in time for her visit, so it was a moot point. Nevertheless, upon reflection I was able to see how my old habit of sympathy and overaccommodation had reflexively showed up without my awareness, blinding me to the timing and correctness of my invitation to her. My intuitive feeling held the truth about the situation and what would be best for all parties involved. As soon as I told my wife of my feeling, she immediately concurred and felt relieved. Our decision had nothing to do with not wanting to see her sister; it was about balance and timing.

Are my thoughts confused, rigid, and habitual, or are they flowing, simple, and clear?

If we observe the quality of our thinking in the moment with conscious awareness, we can sense which source our thoughts are coming from, the true Self or the ego-based thought system. Thoughts from the true Self are insightful, creative, inspired, and clear. They seem to flow like a smooth, running river. Thoughts from the ego-based thought system tend to be strained, effortful, confused, rigid, and committed to a specific outcome or set of beliefs.

In the case of my sister-in-law's potential visit to the cabin, the words, "Of course, we would love to have you," automatically rolled off my tongue. She was delighted and excited about the prospect of seeing us, further confirming the correctness of my response to her. However, something didn't feel right about it. It started to feel like an obligation, complicated, and overwhelming.

I was confused. And so I reflected, *Am I being polite, sympathetic, or genuine? How does the timing feel to have her that week?* I just let these questions rest on the back burner of my mind without trying to force an answer. Consequently, in the middle of my exercise class, the thoughts about my situation began to flow and I knew I had my answer. *Her visit would be three weeks from now and she needs six weeks to receive her permit.* That was the first thought. Next, I thought, *Even if the permit weren't an issue, we still wouldn't have to invite her. She would totally understand. It would give us the special time alone with our other friend.* Last, I recognized in my initial invitation an habitual response—to always be accommodating even if it inconveniences others and myself and is bad timing. This is an example of how discernment of intuition can work in a practical, daily-life situation.

Am I invested in the outcome, or am I open to the wisest answer—regardless of whether or not it disagrees with my past thinking, expectations, or hopes?

When we have a vested interest in getting our way, being in control, or winning, we blind ourselves to what is in our true best interest. The ego blinds us from seeing the path of least resistance, which is usually the right one. We often become invested in doing things the way we have always done them, what fits with our belief system, or what others expect of us. The ego wants to win, to be right, to look good, and to get what we think is just, fair, and right. None of these things may be what is best for us or for all others involved. This is the beauty of intuition— it *knows* all the known and the unknown variables. This knowing is the wisdom we are looking for in discernment.

Political leaders often get caught in this quandary. Rather than admitting that their previous decision or policy was a mistake, they will defend it to the end so as not to appear wishy-washy, out of control, or weak. However, in continuing down the wrong path for the sake of their egos, they further increase the damage of their earlier decisions. By not being courageous enough to admit a mistake, they ultimately lose the people's respect. Backing down often takes more courage and humility than sticking to a past faulty decision out of stubbornness and pride.

We can *feel* when we are invested. Investment in an outcome or an answer feels rigid, self-righteous, controlling, fearful, and unbalanced. Investment prevents us from hearing the voice of intuition, which is why it is another telltale sign of our need to pay attention to our feelings, take time to reflect, and listen to the voice of our true Self.

Am I afraid to hear the truth and avoiding taking time for reflection, or am I courageously facing what life presents me?

Sometimes we ignore the nagging voice of intuition because we are afraid of what we might hear. This is especially true when much of our ego self's sense of security depends on maintaining our current belief system, thus avoiding an often necessary and even positive change.

Several years ago I began to hear the nagging voice of intuition with regard to my professional life. For thirty years I had been a practicing clinical psychologist and made a decent living in my private practice. I was helping people, I was good at it, and my identity (my ego) was tied to it.

For me, the voice of intuition began as a vague dissatisfaction with aspects of the job—insurance forms, resistant clients, feeling trapped by the demands of being available to my clients. However, I could hardly let the thought of not doing something I had trained for much of my life even enter my mind. The vague feeling began to grow into a loud discomfort. I was very puzzled by this feeling, but instead of reflecting on it, I ignored it for two years. In the meantime, I became more attracted to doing seminars, writing, and teaching others to do what I did. When I was engaged in these activities, my heart was full of joy. Still, my ego couldn't imagine letting go of its counselor identity, my steady source of income, and the familiarity of my chosen profession for an unknown risk.

Finally, after two years of avoiding listening to my inner voice on this subject, I decided to go to our cabin and take time to reflect. It was immediately apparent what my heart was telling me: Quit my private practice and take the plunge into teaching and writing. I felt a huge burden lift from my shoulders, and I felt passionate about going back home and closing my office of thirty years to begin a new professional life. The very next month I was awarded a five-year consulting contract with a large hospital system to do training and seminars. Two weeks later, my agent called me to announce that my book had become a best-seller in Japan and my royalties for that year alone would exceed a full year of private counseling. Everything seemed to flow once I listened to the voice of my intuition and had the courage and passion to change. I have never regretted that decision, and it has reinforced for me the power of trusting in that vague, nagging voice of intuition.

Asking yourself these questions will increase your power of discernment. Discerning ego-based thoughts from intuition will connect you to the harmony of living from your true Self.

In the next chapter we explore how not to be swayed by others' fearful stance toward life, and instead how to stay rooted in the true Self and respond with compassion.

REMINDERS

1. Intuition is the clear, flowing, calm voice of the true Self.
2. Intuition acts like radar that sees what is invisible to the other senses.
3. Being present in the moment with a calm mind is the entry point to intuition.
4. The more we trust our intuition, the more we become aware of it.
5. Fear blocks intuition; reflection increases access.

CHAPTER 8
Fearproof
IMMUNITY FROM OTHERS' FEARS

For much of my life I felt like a chameleon, always taking on the feelings of others. I seemed to have no protection from the other person's view of reality. If someone close by was afraid, I became afraid. Most of us strive to have empathy and be sympathetic to others, but I was *too* sympathetic.

As an eighteen-year-old orderly in a psychiatric unit, I would take all my patients' problems home with me and worry about them. Later, as a psychologist and counselor, I sat with people all day whose lives were full of anxiety, anger, depression, paranoia, and a host of other negative mental and emotional states. It wasn't long before I was stressed and, over time, burned out.

I didn't know it at the time, but I was trapped in the world of my ego thought system. Not knowing what else to do, I began to lose my sensitivity and would look at my clients' problems from an intellectual and clinical stance. Becoming distant was the best I could do to protect myself from my clients' emotions. It was also what my supervisors advised me to do. In becoming distant, I thought my counseling skills were improving. In fact, I lost much of my effectiveness as a counselor. I may have felt less vulnerable, but I was also losing the caring and compassion that had originally inspired me to become a psychologist and that was the foundation for the healing quality in my work.

As a result of distancing myself at work, I found myself becoming distant from people outside of work as well. I was no longer the friendly and caring guy I had always been. Inadvertently, I was covering up my innate ability to listen deeply and feel compassion.

It was several more years before I discovered the scientific and spiritual principles by which we create our experience. Only when I realized the power of thought as the source of my experience did I begin to develop immunity to other people's emotions without losing my compassion. Once I realized that my experience of life and all the emotions I was feeling came from the inside out, not the outside in, I felt free to truly care for others again. I found that as I remained in the safety and peace of my true Self, I felt compassion when I was with those who were suffering psychologically. The stress of being a psychotherapist and the resulting burnout became a thing of the past. I could be with others who were in pain and not take it on myself. The protection I learned is precisely what I hope to convey in this chapter.

We are often in the presence of a worrier or an overprotective parent, or sitting next to someone on the plane who is phobic about flying, or reading fear-inducing news stories. How do we immunize ourselves against the fears of others and not take on their realities as our own? A more general question might be: How do we protect ourselves from all the negativity in the world? We live in a world where most people seem to be living in dread of the next epidemic, storm, terrorist attack, or the latest personal issue in their lives. Can we really stay grounded in the peace and wisdom of our true Selves when so many are living in fear and overwhelmed by their efforts to cope with modern life?

In this chapter I tell you how to live in a world full of fear and other forms of negativity and not be harmed by it—*how to be in the world but not of the world*, a principle that I described in chapter 3. You will see that you can experience the joy of compassion, caring, inspired action, and forgiveness. And then you will understand the true meaning of Jesus' words on the cross: "Father forgive them, for they know not what they do." Compassion is love in the presence of suffering.

True compassion makes us fearproof. Compassion cannot be learned, nor is it a skill to be developed. It is the result of understanding how the mind creates all of our experiences in life. Compassion is a by-product of living in our true Selves. When we are connected to our true essence, we realize that we are a part of all that exists. We come to understand our own innocence and see that we were living under the tyranny of the ego and were unaware of its destructive and self-defeating grip on our lives. As we see our own innocent addiction to habitual thought and our identification with it, we realize that everyone is in the same boat. This understanding makes it easier to realize how people can do such seemingly ignorant and cruel things. It doesn't mean we passively respond to them and become a doormat, but it does take away our judgment of them, thus freeing us of fear and anger and allowing us to take appropriate action. We understand that seeing the innocence in others and ourselves does not mean we are not responsible for our actions or that cruel or ignorant actions are acceptable.

In this chapter I describe six guidelines to protect us from the fears of others:

1. Stay grounded in presence and Being.
2. Don't take what others are doing personally.
3. See the innocence of others.
4. Feel compassion by understanding separate realities.
5. Shake it off.
6. Take right action.

Stay Grounded in Presence and Being

Staying grounded in our true Selves keeps us in a state of profound presence and awareness. Being grounded means that we are actually living from the true Self—not just *believing* that it is a good idea. We are congruent with our Being. We are an embodiment of the truth of who we are. This security in who we are is like a tree whose roots are firmly planted in the ground, able to withstand strong winds of adversity. It keeps us from entering other persons' "reality" and taking on the resulting feelings of fear and anxiety they are experiencing. Staying grounded in our true Selves prevents us from triggering our own thought system similarities to the other person's thoughts and commiserating with their predicament. Instead, we relate to their innate Spirit that has the power to transcend the situation and see solutions.

When a child is frightened by the dark, the natural parental response is to reassure the child, hold them with affection, and remain calm while they are upset. Most parents don't take on their child's irrational fears. Over time the child will lose his fear of the dark through persistent, calm reassurance from his parents.

This same principle applies to adult situations. For many years I worked with hospitals and clinics to teach health care professionals how to remain calm with patients who were extremely emotional or in life-threatening situations. I taught these professionals how to "be with" the person in pain by *listening deeply* to them, feeling compassion, and then doing their jobs (mending a wound, performing a surgery, administering medication). Over the course of time, the level of staff burnout and stress decreased significantly while patient satisfaction reports went up dramatically. Of course, the hospital always intended to be a caring institution, but under extreme stress the staff had lost their bearings (grounding). From that negative state of mind, the staff ignored their patients, became calloused, quit listening, and lost most of their compassion. Because they judged their patients and took their emotional states personally, the staff had no immunity from patients' negativity. They suffered from what is now a popular term in medical circles—"compassion fatigue." By empowering themselves through understanding how they and everyone else creates their experience via their thinking, they were able to return to the caring people they had been before they became burned out.

The staff at the hospital I worked with also became immune to other staff members' negativity. They discovered how not to get caught up in the gossip that was always flying around the conference rooms. By remaining in their true Selves, they were able to listen compassionately to their coworkers. They also knew when to walk away and not participate in the gossip and fearful projections so common in these types of institutions. The entire culture shifted from one of negativity, stress, and anger to one of calm, caring, and compassion.

Like the hospital personnel, we have the ability to be with others who are in a state of fear or other negative emotional states and not catch their "mental flu." Remaining grounded in our true Selves allows us to listen deeply and feel compassion when we are with others who are in pain without sacrificing our healthy state of balance.

Don't Take It Personally

Yesterday I was at a stoplight waiting for the light to turn green. The elderly man in front of me was preoccupied with looking at something and didn't see that the light had changed. After ten seconds or so I honked my horn to get his attention. Based on the way he reacted to me, I could see he took my action as a personal judgment and insult. He refused to move and glared at me. He then swerved in front of my car when I tried to get ahead (and away) from him. He appeared drunk. At the next stoplight, my wife, who was in the passenger seat, was alongside him and spoke to him from her window, trying to reassure him that my honking at him meant no harm. He persisted in his anger and self-righteous behavior. At that point I could see he was not open to changing his view.

My first thought was, *What a jerk!* However, before I drove off I looked at his face I could see this was a very troubled man, and my heart went out to him. I realized his reaction to me had nothing personal in it. He was mad at the world, at least the day I saw him. Who knows what else was going on in his head or in his world? It doesn't really matter. What did matter was my reaction to him. I had a choice: *Do I take his behavior personally and let it ruin my day, or do I see it for what it is—the product of a human being who is caught up in his personal ego world of thought?* Once a person is caught up in that personal ego world of thought, he projects onto others whatever his fears and insecurities are.

If I didn't know what I know now, I probably would have reacted to him as I had in the past and let the experience ruin my day and harden my view of people. Many people in this world are unhappy, and if we take personally the actions of each unhappy person we encounter, we will become one of them.

Which will you choose?

Taking people personally is the result of not knowing that each person is innocently creating his or her separate view of reality from unconscious thought. We assume that people are aware of what they are doing and are just "stupid," "crazy," "lazy," "evil," and/or a host of other negative labels. *These labels are the result of our own ignorance, not theirs.* It is easy to forget this in the moment, as I did at the traffic light that day. If, however, we can pause in our reaction and take responsibility for the reality we are creating by taking people personally, we are free to rechoose how we see and respond to them.

I often ask people if they are going to charge rent to the perceptions of people they are allowing to live in their head and ruin their day. When we realize we are the landlords of our own inner world, we are more likely to take responsibility for our own response.

See Innocence

If I had gone with my ego's reaction to the man in the car, I may have had a dangerous confrontation with him. At the very least, I would have gotten very upset about the fact that people like him exist in the world, how unfair his reaction to me was, how the world was going to hell in a hand basket, and how he was just more evidence of it! All of these reactions would have triggered my habitual emotional response of stress, anger, and judgment.

It would have ruined my day, but it didn't. Instead, after the thought *What a jerk!* went through my head, something shifted inside me. I had a moment of awareness, my inner intelligence of wisdom came into consciousness. Then, something else within me kicked in: *I saw his innocence.* I realized he wasn't my enemy, just an old, sad man at odds with the world and taking it out on someone who honked at him. My heart went out to him.

If I had continued with my original judgment, I would have created a nasty set of feelings in my body and spread them to my wife and anyone else who would have listened. This is the power of seeing innocence. It immunizes us against other's pain and negativity. We all have this capacity to recognize innocence when we listen inside to the voice of our true Selves speaking to us and warning us of the path we are about to go down if we continue with the ego's habitual response.

The saying, "There but by the grace of God go I," has relevance here. We are all capable of reacting like the old man I spoke of earlier, if we are upset enough, stressed out sufficiently, or just in a very low mood. We can easily forget that fact when we encounter someone who is having a bad day or perhaps much worse and acting like we do on occasion. Judgmental people tend to be the ones who are hardest on other judgmental people. Isn't that interesting?

Seeing innocence does not mean that we lose awareness of when someone is potentially harmful to others or us. It simply decreases our suffering and allows us to be in the world but not of it. Seeing innocence doesn't mean you don't send people to alcoholism treatment or jail or fire them from your workplace. It just means you don't lose sight of their humanity and your response to their pain. I am not recommending inaction, as I address in a moment when I talk about taking right action. I am simply suggesting that seeing innocence protects *you* from the pain you inflict on yourself in reaction to others' pain.

The opposite of seeing innocence is being judgmental. How does it feel when you are judgmental of others or even of yourself? Does it feel all warm and fuzzy? No, it feels sickening. Judgment separates us from humanity. It is a trick of the ego to feel superior. The ego constantly needs to be fed with the reassurance that it is okay, and one way to do that is to feel superior to others. When we feel inferior we try to prove that we aren't; sometimes by pointing out faults in others or trying to intimidate them so we feel more powerful. Bullies are an excellent example of this principle. This is a battle—proving it is worthy—that the ego will never win. We are already worthy—worthy of love, respect, and happiness—without being superior to others. Being judgmental only satisfies the ego for a moment and never brings us true happiness or self-esteem. Don't be fooled by your ego for a moment of false superiority. See judgment and feelings of superiority as the caution light on the dashboard, warning you that you are caught up in your ego thinking.

Feel Compassion

Compassion is a by-product of staying grounded in the true Self, not taking other people personally, and seeing their innocence. Our natural humanity shines through when we can set aside our ego and recognize the filter of judgment-based conditioning. Concepts of good and bad, right and wrong, moral and immoral, sane and crazy all stem from the ego-based thought system. Compassion is the feeling of love that prevents judgment. It releases a positive feeling that is healing both to the person feeling it and to those on the receiving end.

As I spoke of in chapter 4, "Creators of Experience," we all live in a thought-created world, mostly born of habits learned from our parents, our culture, and other social influences. Our habitual, judgmental conditioning is as unquestioned and invisible to us as water is to a fish. Yet our thought system, whether or not we are aware of it, is the cause of all of our perceptions.

Our thought system acts like an invisible filter or lens through which we view each and every experience of our lives. Unconsciously, our thought system informs our senses of what to selectively perceive, judge, expect, fear, and then respond to, based on those perceptions.

Once we have conscious awareness that all of us are doing precisely the same thing, compassion is an automatic result. *Intellectually knowing* this principle only creates another belief, but *realizing* this principle of separate realities leads to a true understanding of the human condition.

A word of caution: The ego is clever enough to take any of our insights and turn it into an ego belief—if we let it. For example, when we first become aware that we are creating our own experience, we may sometimes be quick to judge others for not understanding the principle of separate realities. We may be equally quick to judge ourselves when we momentarily lose awareness that we are thinking, perceiving, and creating our behavior. When we judge others, we punish ourselves with the feelings of anger, disgust, bigotry, and resentment. These are some of the judgment games the ego plays in turning an insight into an ego belief. We don't have to keep playing, though. We need only remind ourselves that when we are disconnected from the true Self, it is easy to forget the innocence of others and ourselves. Then we take a moment, reconnect, and remember.

Shake It Off

When I played hockey, opponents would often try to check me in an attempt to trigger my ego defenses and cause me to retaliate. If I fell for the tactic, I would lose my bearings and my game would suffer. My coach would always tell us to "shake it off" and get back in the game. Hockey players know that when a player is angry and upset, his playing ability suffers, which is why they often try to taunt and irritate the other players. The thought of the check captivates the targeted player's focus, blocking his awareness of the continuing game. The coach would always pull the upset player to the bench until he could regain his bearings. Those who were good at "shaking it off" could get back in the game more quickly.

As we go through life, it is inevitable that we will run into people who are frightened, angry, judgmental, impolite, cruel, and in many other negative ego states. It is also inevitable that at some time or another we will be affected by those people, taking their actions personally no matter how much we know about the mind and the nature of experience. This is where the principle of shaking it off is essential.

Birds are great teachers of how to shake it off. At my house I often see birds hit the picture window and become stunned and sometimes even unconscious for a few minutes. However, they eventually regain consciousness, get to their feet, and shake their feathers and whole body wildly. Then their feathers smooth out and off they go, flying away to the woods. It doesn't ruin their day, and they don't fume about it with their fellow birds, at least to my knowledge. They just go on with their lives.

Like birds, we can shake it off after we have reacted to other people and lost our bearings.

Here are a few guidelines for shaking it off and getting back to your center.

- Don't judge yourself for reacting, and don't blame the other person for your reaction.
- Allow any emotions to surface, be aware of them, don't judge them, and let them go.
- Be in the present. We only have the present moment in which to live. Remember that you are no longer in the past moment when the event occurred.
- The past is only a thought carried through time by memory. Thoughts can't hurt you unless you take them as reality.

Take Right Action

Sometimes, when you are with others who are in a fearful state, feeling compassion is insufficient for the situation. Although compassion is the immune agent to protect you spiritually and emotionally from harming yourself with what others are doing and feeling, at times you will need to take action. The Buddhists have a term for acting from your true Self. They call it "right action." When we are with others who are operating from their ego-based fearful state, be they children, a coworker, a spouse, or a terrorist, it is imperative that we stay grounded in our true Self; in so doing we will know whether we are to accept the situation or the person or if we are to take some action to protect ourselves, others, or the person themselves from harmful or hostile action.

Taking right action usually does not require preconception or planning. Right action often arises out of the situation as an instinctual response from our true Self. (Of course there are times that right action takes the form of planning for some future event.)

I remember hearing a news story a number of years ago about an ordinary person performing a very heroic deed. A man was driving on the bridge over the Potomac River when a helicopter crashed into the water. He immediately stopped his car and jumped off the bridge into the freezing February waters. In the process, he saved many lives and became an instant national hero. He was interviewed by all the major media and his humble response was, "I didn't do anything extraordinary; you would have done the same thing."

He wasn't saying this to act humble—he really meant it. He was as surprised as anyone at how he acted. He didn't think; he just jumped in the river and saved as many people as he could.

I would say that his compassion kicked in, and he responded to the tragedy that was in front of him. His story is one of countless stories about ordinary people performing extraordinary acts of courage in the midst of war, natural disasters, criminal assaults, and vehicle accidents. In fact, people often recall being in horrible circumstances and having a powerful feeling of calm come over them, and with it a surprising, superhuman strength to do *right action*. When we perform right action, we know it is appropriate to the situation because it arises from the intelligence, wisdom, and common sense of the true Self.

Many years ago I worked as a consultant with a hospital system in Michigan. I was training their staff in the principles we have talked about in this book. A nurse at one of my trainings told a story that illustrates the importance of a calm mind and right action. She was part of a "code blue" team, which is a term for the coronary response team in a hospital. During the previous week, the team had responded to a heart attack in the ER. Initially, they were at cross-purposes—everyone was in a panic, tripping over one another while working frantically trying to save the patient's life. The patient was going to die if they didn't get it together. Out of the blue she remembered to clear her thoughts and get calm. She then screamed to the group, "Calm down and get your bearings!" They all knew she was right; without hesitation they cleared their heads. As a result, the team worked like a well-oiled machine and saved the woman's life.

In our daily lives we have many opportunities each day to operate from our true Selves and perform right action in the presence of others who are full of fear and other forms of ego-based negativity, even if it is just a rude driver, someone pushing ahead in line at the grocery store, or our child having a temper tantrum in the middle of Target. It may be as simple as not reacting to them from our ego or as powerful as a kind smile and asking if we can help. It may mean taking Johnny out of the store and bringing him home for a nap. It may be (and often is) taking no action—just the power of staying centered in your true Self is a powerful response, if for no one else but yourself. The right action will occur to you in the moment from the wisdom of your true Self.

As we enter this era of unprecedented change and transformation, we will have ample opportunities to practice these guidelines for dealing with others who are in a state of insecurity and negativity. As you become ever more aware of your moments of choice when you are reacting from your ego, perhaps these guidelines will come to mind as an alternative.

The final two chapters of this books serve as a means to pull together all the principles and concepts presented and to show you how to transform the fearlessness of living from the true Self into inspired action. They will show you how to live in a world where fear has become the norm as an agent of inspiration, change, and peace. Chapter 10 provides guideposts that recap the book and also serve as encouragement to live from these guideposts.

REMINDERS

1. Compassion is love in the presence of suffering—it is the path to becoming fearproof.
2. Compassion is a by-product of staying grounded in our true Self, not taking others' egos personally, and seeing the innocence of others.
3. Guidelines for protecting ourselves from the fears of others:
   - Stay grounded in presence and Being.
   - Don't take what others are doing personally.
   - See the innocence of others.
   - Feel compassion by understanding separate realities.
   - Shake it off.
   - Take right action.
4. Labeling others as crazy, stupid, and lazy is the result of our ignorance, not theirs.
5. Being immune to other's fears does not mean being passive. Take right action.

CHAPTER 9
Transforming Fearlessness into Right Action

By using the principles in this book, everyone can break their addiction to fear and begin to live a life connected to and guided by their true Self: a fearproof life. But how does our personal journey influence the lives of those around us and our world as a whole? As we look at the larger issues of the world, the same choice is before each of us: the path of fear, or the path of courage and change. Will we transform our world from one of fear to one of empowerment and peace? Will we let the forces of the ego cripple us, or will we be our fullest true Selves? Will we transform the imbalances, injustices, and dangers we face into opportunities to express ourselves honestly and totally, and thus improve our world?

One of my favorite quotes about this is by Nelson Mandela (who is actually quoting Marianne Williamson).

Our deepest fear is not that we are inadequate. Our deepest fear is that we are powerful beyond measure. It is our light, not our darkness that most frightens us. Your playing small does not serve the world. There is nothing enlightened about shrinking so that other people won't feel insecure around you. We are all meant to shine as children do. It's not just in some of us, it's in everyone. And as we let our own light shine we unconsciously give other people permission to do the same. As we are liberated from our own fear, our presence automatically liberates others.

Nelson Mandela's life is certainly a poignant example of his own quote. As he sat in a South African prison, he had a vision to stop apartheid in his country, not by violence, but by taking back the power and forgiving his oppressors. Through his conviction, vision, and courage he transformed an entrenched system of oppression by just being true to his Self and inspiring a whole nation and eventually the world to support his efforts.

There are many visionaries throughout history who have done the same—Jesus, Mohammad, the Buddha, Gandhi, and Martin Luther King Jr. Each of them was just like each of us, meaning we all have the potential for deep insight from our true Self; the difference is that they trusted and acted on it. Some fully realized their true Selves to the degree of enlightenment; others tapped into it and had moments of pure inspiration, mixed with moments of ego. Whether it was one moment, many moments, or a lifetime of allowing their pure Spirit to guide and to express, their examples show that acting from the power of the true Self is possible for every human being, and the results are beneficial for the whole.

It is not only famous historical figures who have followed the path of the true Self and courage in a moment of awareness. The Berlin Wall fell because thousands of anonymous individuals simultaneously took to the streets to tear it down, overwhelming the military authorities. They chose the path of courage and the true Self over the path of fear, and their iconoclastic strength overcame the entrenched regime. Nevertheless, courage rarely feels like courage at the time to the person doing the "right action." They are simply doing the thing that makes sense at that moment, from their Spirit. To others their acts look heroic, courageous, and even superhuman. They are being themselves fully— that is all.

The path of inspired action sometimes is wrapped in unexpected packages. Shortly after Israel attacked Lebanon in 2006 in retaliation for the kidnapping of two soldiers, I read an article about how this situation could easily turn into a world war. That night I was awakened by a fearful dream about the war in the Middle East.

I awoke with a feeling of dread about the war in Iraq and the expanding regional war between Israel and Hezbollah. The fear left me feeling anxious, tense, and unable to sleep. I was at a crossroads lying there in bed—should I ignore the fear and try to go back to sleep, or should I discover if there was a purpose to my dream and, if so, what should do about it? Many times in my life I have rolled over and gone back to sleep by simply recognizing my fearful thoughts as thoughts and letting them go. It is appropriate to deal with many of our fears in this manner. But it is also wise to find out, from our Divine perspective, if we need to hear something more deeply or take action. In the case of my dream, the voice in my head said, *Get up and do something; your fear has a purpose.*

I made myself a cup of tea, sat down with my journal, and asked my true Self about this dream and my fear. What I heard was that its purpose was to inspire me to write this chapter. It wasn't enough for me to recognize my fear and let it go, thus returning to a state of fearlessness; I needed to take inspired action. In this case, writing about transforming fearlessness into right action *was* the right action. I know this because I have ultimate confidence in my true Self to guide me under these circumstances. I know to trust my Self and listen deeply to its wise guidance.

As you know by now, I didn't always feel guided by my true Self. I spent my early life living in fear, addicted to thinking about all my worries, stresses, and concerns, not knowing that I had the inner resource of my true Self. Fear immobilized me and kept me from acting on my dreams, desires, and inspirations. As I discovered how to live a fearless life from my true Self, I found that it wasn't enough just to be fearless. I also needed to have courage—courage to act on a hunch, courage to speak the truth even when it made others uncomfortable or I risked a friendship or approval, and courage to move past the limitations of my habitual belief system.

Many times we wake up momentarily to our true Selves and take action, not really recognizing why we feel that strength and conviction, not really seeing that it is who we really are. The next moment, we again disconnect from our true Selves, and the memory of inspiration becomes a fleeting dream. We might then turn our insight into an ironclad belief about how to handle certain situations and ignore our wisdom in the moment. Many religious, political, and familial beliefs start this way. I remember hearing my sister ask my mom why she cut the ham in half for Easter every year. She responded with, *That's the way Mama always did it.* It turned out Grandma didn't have a big enough pan and that was her way of solving the once-a-year ham dilemma. It's so easy to fall back asleep; we do it many times a day—that is, if we're lucky. For most, waking up at all is a rare occurrence.

We are at a critical time in history when in order for our planet and species to survive, the forces of the true Self and courage must replace the forces of fear and the ego. This requires transformation of each individual, one by one. We have the power to make this choice. The question is, will you?

A World That Has Lost Its Bearings

Every generation since the beginning has felt the burden of fear. We have always lived in fear, and fear has always had adverse effects on how we relate to each other and the planet.

However, with the technological revolution, the information age, and the dawning of weapons of mass destruction, fear becomes more lethal and has greater and faster consequences for more people than ever before. Through mass transit and air travel, disease can spread around the planet in weeks or months rather than decades. A nuclear bomb in the hands of a deranged leader of a rogue nation or a major world leader acting from fear can destroy an entire civilization from across the globe in minutes. Fear-inducing news with high-definition images comes to us in real time over the cable news networks and the Internet.

The growing world economy, though it promises the sharing of the "good life" of materialism, is hastening the destruction of the planet through pollution of our air, water, and land and the resulting global climate change. We are out of balance—with our bodies, our consumption of world resources, our ecology, and our ability to get along as a diverse group of human beings sharing the same beautiful planet Earth. When we approach our problems from the ego self, we create self-destructive behaviors on an individual and societal scale.

The Collective Unconsciousness

In Aldous Huxley's classic 1932 novel, *Brave New World,* he described a futuristic society whose citizens are completely controlled by a totalitarian worldwide organization whose motto— "Community, Identity, Stability"—summarizes its mission. If citizens ever experience any discomfort or negative emotion, they immediately receive a dose of the pill "soma," which returns them to a state of compliant tranquility and thus preserves the stability of the society.

Have we become, in this early part of the twenty-first century, a version of the society that Huxley predicted? No one is giving us "soma," we might reassure ourselves, and there is no totalitarian state controlling our minds, although some conspiracy theorists may disagree with this conclusion. Nevertheless, I believe we *are* being controlled—not by some external force, but by our *collective unconsciousness.*

The tyranny we live under is the tyranny of the mind—a mind addicted to our ego thought system that generates thoughts and feelings of fear. The "soma" pill we take is our addiction to our distractions from fear. These distractions may take various forms: consumerism, addiction to food, obsession with body image, success, money, television, the Internet, power, alcohol, drugs, and anything else that blocks our awareness of our fear. We live in a world of background noise, an invisible fear that has us hypnotized by the past and the future, unaware of the reality of the present moment. This is the collective unconsciousness.

Our addiction to fear is as insidious as a hidden camera or phone and e-mail eavesdropping system. The ego is blinding us with fear to keep us from seeing what is our true birthright—the truth of our Divine nature, the true Self. In addition, by filling our minds with so many competing fears, most of which are imagined and illusionary, we have made our minds numb with fear and/or distractions and have become unable to discern *real dangers* from the contrived. Through our mass addiction to the media (of all types) we have lost touch with what is truly important to our survival as a species and our ability to enjoy life.

The media has mastered the art of manipulation of people's behavior through advertising and uses entertainment, news, sports, or anything else to sell us products and create desire for "things" that are absolutely unnecessary for our well-being or survival. They know just how to select the perfect "hook" that lies within us, whether it is the archetypal desire to live, love, and feel fulfilled or the fear of death and extinction. Naturally, mass communication knows just how to hone and develop the skill of persuasion beyond any individual sophistication.

The human condition of the ego makes us susceptible to the influences of others. Our ego is, in a sense, fighting all the time for its survival—trying to justify its beliefs of reality, trying to get others to join with it and validate its beliefs by ignoring anything or anyone that disrupts the status quo. Truth has a hard time entering into the picture when the ego is the bouncer at the door. This is especially true when our family, friends, our community, and our culture validate the collectively held belief system that is based on illusion. To hear the truth above the roar of the ego thought system takes courage, deep listening, and a commitment to live from the true Self.

An Internal Revolution

Could we still obtain the good life (or better) if we let go of our old thinking and relied on spiritual insight? I believe so—there are dreams to be dreamt and infinite possibilities to explore when we unleash the creative forces of the true Self.

The only real plausible solution to the world we face today is to live from our spiritual core—the true Self. It is only when we change our own individual consciousness that we can change the consciousness of humanity. It is only when we live from the true Self that we can think and act in a way that leads to peace, health, respect, justice, and balance of nature and humanity. Imagine what the world would be like if everyone started living from the true Self. Nations would find creative ways to end wars through innovative diplomacy based on mutual respect, not on the failed tendencies of revenge and more violence that only continues to escalate.

We must start somewhere—and it must begin with each of us. It is only when we as individuals develop this latent potential in ourselves to live as spiritual beings in the world that we will be immune from the pushers of fear whose aim is to control our minds, our behavior, and our freedom. When we become free-thinking Beings exercising our power of choice, we challenge the collective unconsciousness, often called the status quo, which tries to pressure us to conform to the rules and mores of a society, even when those ideas are rooted in illusion.

It is only when we are living from our true Selves that we will have the courage, intelligence, and wisdom to create a brave new world.

The Brave New World

The brave new world I speak of is created from the fearlessness of the Self and knows no division or enemies. This brave new world is the budding of human consciousness—the waking up of humanity to the realization of its true spiritual identity. This brave new world is a time of true freedom from our addiction to fear and a new understanding of fear as a vehicle for reawakening us when we have fallen asleep at the wheel of life.

As humankind wakes up from the collective unconsciousness and we loosen the chains of our addiction to fear, there is a quiet but progressive revolution on Earth. Gradually, the fear tactics of fanatical leaders, be they religious, political, or media pundits, will no longer take root in the fearful masses. The fear pushers will no longer be able to fool their audiences. As we discover how to discern the voice of the ego from the true Self, we will be immune to fear tactics meant to separate us from one another and from our true Selves. We will discover that oneness is truth. We are all born of the same God, the same human Spirit, and we are no longer each other's enemy, foe, or competitor. We *are* a brave new world—one where we no longer fear an external image of God, each other, or ourselves.

In this brave new world we see how to support unity, oneness, and common ground, not division. Our fearless world is one of peace, harmony, celebrated differences, respect for truth and beauty of each individual, of each expression of Divine creation. We are liberators of the Spirit—not of nations, groups, or other social identities, but liberators of the Self that lies within each soul of humanity.

How can this inner revolution of consciousness occur? What are the choices we face that will take us down this road of awakening? What guideposts can we turn to in order to facilitate this transformation of humankind from a world of the self-destructive, ego-bound habits to a brave new world born of the Divine Self in each of us?

How do we begin to apply the principles in this book to the larger issues that face us in the world today?

CHAPTER 10
Living IN The World, but Not OF the World—Fearlessly

How do you express your true Self in the world? How do you remain true to your Self in a way that is respectful, courageous, wise, and supportive to the Spirit of others—your family, your community, your country, and your world? Where do you find the courage to do so? How do you put all of the principles of this book into practice? How do you live courageously in the world but not be at the effect of it?

This last chapter of the book is both a summary of the key points of the book and a call to inspired action that will show you how to create a brave new world that starts with your own personal transformation, a world that is born of the true Self, not the ego. The ultimate cure for your addiction to fear is to act from the true Self—and transform fearlessness into action.

The Art of Personal Evolution

We tend to think that once we choose to be on the path of personal transformation and a fearless life that it will be a seamless transition and we will be happy from here ever after. Making the choice to live from our true Self instead of the fear-based ego self is a turning point, but it is not a straight line of change.

Personal evolution is often two steps forward, and what appears to be one step backward. If we don't understand the process and the art of personal evolution, we can become discouraged and judge ourselves for not being "perfect." It is with this in mind that I close this book with some cautionary notes about this process and a summary of the key guidelines that have been presented in the book to aid us in staying on the path of our true Self.

I like to describe this process of personal evolution as a circular spiral, always going up toward more awareness, more love, and more peace. However, within the stages of this spiral, old habits of fear and our ego thought system resurface just when we think we have conquered our old habitual patterns. Why is this?

The visitation of an old habit gives us the opportunity to correct an old choice made from an earlier level of consciousness when we were unaware of our thinking. The next time an old ego habit appears, do not view it as a sign of failure, recognize it as a moment of choice; this is the path of true and permanent change. From this new level of awareness we see the habit from the observer state with insight, acceptance, and understanding.

This is a natural process that allows us to eliminate all that is not our true Self. Each time an old habit arises, if we are willing, open, and have humility, we will glean more insight about how we innocently accepted a belief that is in conflict with who we truly are. With increased insight we shift to a higher level of consciousness and from that vantage point we are aware of more choice, more freedom, and are able to more consistently live in the realm of our true Self.

Figure 7 illustrates this process of personal evolution.

It is important to understand this process so that you don't become discouraged in your evolutionary process. I still have remnants of the same habitual thoughts I have always had, but when I reexperience those habitual patterns of thought I more quickly see them for what they are—habits of my false sense of self, the ego. Then I am able to more readily choose the path of my true Self and forgive myself for "slipping" back into old patterns. Each time, I gain more clarity, more resolve, more understanding of how to stay on the path.

Figure 7 THE SPIRALS OF FEAR ADDICTION AND PERSONAL EVOLUTION

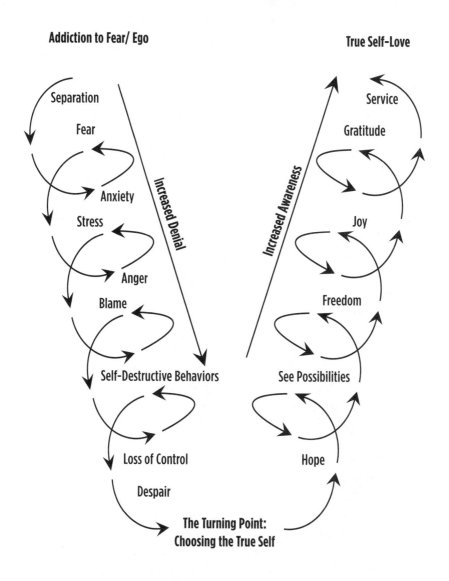

It is not how often one falls back into the past that is relevant, but how one relates to that falling back. If we understand that it is but another opportunity to go deeper in our understanding, then we will raise our awareness, have insights, and move on. If we judge ourselves and become discouraged, we will stay stuck in self-judgment and guilt.

The Twelve Guidelines to Living in the True Self

The following guidelines are offered to encourage and inspire you to live in the world as your true Self and, in so doing, inspire others to do the same and to be an agent of positive change in the world.

1. Know thy Self (true Self versus ego).
2. Be your Self.
3. Be true to your Self.
4. Honor your true Self and its unique expression.
5. Listen to the voice of truth through reflection and deep listening.
6. Trust your insights, intuition, inspiration, and wisdom.
7. Transform Spirit into form through courage to act from the true Self.
8. Beware of your ego taking credit (symptoms: pride, superiority, judgment, control).
9. Be willing to act from your true Self, even when others don't understand or approve.
10. Forgive yourself when you slip back into ego habits.
11. Forgive others for their ego-based actions by seeing their innocence and the illusion of separate realities.
12. Take responsibility for whatever you create.

Know Thy Self (True Self versus Ego)

As I discussed in the chapters 1 and 2, we all come into this world with the purity of our true Self, but through misunderstanding, we wrongly think we are separate from our Divine Source. This misconception forms the basis for the illusionary ego self that becomes our false identity. Our personality and all its traits, beliefs, concepts, limitations, prejudices, qualities, and defects are maintained and perpetuated through the ego thought system. This in turn forms our separate reality and is the root of all our personal fears and all the conflicts in the world. There are also larger thought systems of societies, groups, and cultures. These collectively form what is known as the collective unconscious. Knowing yourself is not about analyzing your personality and discovering the root of your psychological history and pathology. I spent much of my career learning to diagnose, evaluate, and "fix" dysfunctional addictions and mental illnesses by trying to change something (the ego) that wasn't real in the first place. This psychological fad of self-help and self-analysis or professional help, though sometimes helpful, is for the most part a distraction from knowing the true Self.

It is only by going within through reflection, insight, and wisdom that you come to know the true Self. The true Self is your true identity, your spiritual nature. When you glimpse it, you experience profound feelings of awe, peace, joy, and understanding. When you choose to live from your true Self, you have a life of true peace of mind and happiness.

Through the power of discernment you are able to recognize when you are living from the ego or the true Self. Your internal sensations—your emotions—act as signals to alert you to when you are operating from your ego thoughts or from your Universal Intelligence. This internal alarm clock is there to wake you up to when fear has taken over. The clock's purpose is not to stay on; that would create stress. Its purpose is to wake you up so that you may reflect and hear your inner voice.

The result of living from your true Self is a life in which you act and behave in alignment with your Divine nature. You are in harmony with your body, yourself, other people, and the planet. You experience a state of confidence and certainty that allows you to move through the world in an empowered way and creates success in all aspects of your life.

Be Your Self

Once you've glimpsed your Spirit and chosen that state of consciousness, it's time to live there. Being your Self is an experience, not a concept. When you are with someone who is trying to *act* like him or herself, that person often seems phony or hypocritical. Being you is natural, easy, and flows from within. It is not an intellectual belief of who you should or shouldn't be. On the contrary, it is not acting at all—it is just *being you*. Young children are an example of this ease. They are not trying to prove anything or compete for victory; they are just enjoying life. Being your Self is *relaxing* into who you are.

The process of becoming your true Self is transformational in nature. As you gradually become aware of when you have fallen back into ego habits and fear, you needn't feel bad about this or guilty. Transformation from the ego to the true Self requires awareness without judgment → acceptance → choice. Through awareness you are able to discern when you are back in old ego habits by the *feeling* of your thoughts and your emotions. Accepting your momentary loss of consciousness and just seeing that you are in a process of becoming who you are enables you to let go of your attachment to the outcome or doing everything "right." Remembering that you are not your habits allows you to stop identifying with the ego and instead align with your spiritual core—your true Self. When you are being your true Self, you are aligned with Universal Intelligence.

Being aligned with Universal Intelligence unites you with the essence of each person in the world. Few are consciously aware of their connection to it, but when you speak and act from your true Self, there is recognition from others that you are speaking the truth. This is what gave people like Gandhi and Martin Luther King Jr. such influence in the world. They didn't have political power, economic power, or military might. What they had was the spiritual power of truth, and this in turn inspired millions to join with them in their cause for justice and love. They were *being* their true Selves.

Be True to Your Self

Being true to your Self is the result of knowing your Self, listening to your Self, and having the courage and integrity to follow the truth of your heart.

Sometimes it's obvious when you're not following your heart, but you do it anyway. It may be a time when you're afraid someone will think less of you, or that you'll inconvenience them or hurt their feelings. We usually think of these times as innocuous, but they're not.

When you feel that "tug" from your Self, no matter how small, it's time to reflect. Surprisingly, the little things usually point to a larger, invisible ego belief that keeps you from being true to your Self in many areas of your life. The invisible belief is unconscious; thus, you repeatedly choose the belief over the wisdom of your Self.

For example, recently my friend Jessie asked me about a misunderstanding she was having with another friend. We could have talked about the details and come up with a strategy of how she could handle the "annoying" situation; that was what she was looking for. But it was obvious that all her proper strategies had not worked. I told her to forget about her friend and the situation; this was an opportunity to see something deeper about her.

I recommended that Jessie ask for her Divine point of view. Was there a belief that she might have about friendship, a code she aspired to that she thought noble and proper that she applied to each and every situation, regardless of the moment? I told her I've noticed sometimes that what I think is one of my virtues turns out to be just another ego belief with a noble cover, like blind loyalty or always giving someone the benefit of the doubt. Jessie realized that in her definition of friendship, she was required to accept her friend totally, even when the friend's behavior affected her in a negative way. For example, Jessie's friend is a heavy smoker, and even though she has requested that she not smoke when with her, she still does and she politely doesn't say anything because she wants to respect her friend's preferences. She realized that she could be loving and respectful to her friend and still be respectful to herself, so she had a conversation with her about the smoking.

If, on the surface, all seems well even though you may feel that tug of insight telling you differently, it is time to take time to listen. No matter how well meaning you may be, if you are not listening to your true Self, you are doing just that, *not listening*—which means you are not being true to your Self. Giving someone the "benefit of the doubt" when they are acting against their true Self—just because you're trying to live up to your ego identity of a "nice person"—is not helpful to anyone. Noticing what is true is not being judgmental.

Being true to your Self is a goal to always have on your radar screen—with that in mind your discernment level will rise measurably. Through experience you will not take your true Self for granted; you'll be willing to check in and find out if you are listening to your true Self or allowing yourself to remain in the status quo. Ask questions and act on your Divine answers.

When you are not true to your Self you are not free. When you aren't free, you suffer, and the world suffers for its loss of you. Being true to our Selves is what makes men and women great and successful. It is what allows us to make a contribution to society, our families, and our own happiness. Most human beings in their old age regret not having followed their dreams, taking risks, and saying what was on their mind to those closest to them.

You need not end up being full of regrets, because you are free to choose your life.

Honor Your True Self and Its Unique Expression

No two people are alike, as no two snowflakes are the same. We all have a very special purpose here in this life. Some of us are meant to be healers, some are meant to lead countries, others are best suited to be parents, some love to fight fires and be policemen, others love science and the discovery of seemingly insignificant things. When you honor your gifts and dreams and dare to follow them, you are fulfilling your unique, Divine purpose on Earth.

When you fulfill your purpose and express your unique Self in the world, you are enriched. The same is true of cultures and countries. Each culture has something of value to offer to the whole. When you respect and honor that uniqueness, you are enriched. I love to travel to different cultures and discover what their unique contribution to the planet is—their art, architecture, food, language, books, landscapes, music, customs, their unique way of being in the world. Each contribution is a treasure to hold in love and respect. Remember that the world of the ego is a world of comparing, judging what is different, competing for resources, recognition, and power. If you truly honor your Self, you will be able to honor others. It is only the insecure who feel the need to judge others. When you love yourself, you easily love others.

When I was in India a few years ago giving seminars to businesses, I was initially shocked and depressed by the level of poverty and the disparity between the very rich and the very poor. However, I noticed that the poor, though certainly suffering from lack of shelter and food, were seemingly rich in Spirit. They greet each other with the word *Namaste*, which loosely translates as "From the God in me to the God in you." The Hindus recognize that each of us is Divinity in form.

Jesus said it another way: "Whatsoever you do to the least of my brethren, you do unto me." This wisdom is an expression of the common purpose we all have—to honor our uniqueness and the uniqueness of everyone else. If more people heeded these words, we would have peace throughout the world.

Listen to the Voice of Truth through Reflection and Deep Listening

In our culture of high-speed Internet, multi-tasking, sound-bite news, and a high-stress lifestyle, time is at a premium. The thought of taking time for your Self—to reflect, relax, and listen within to your wisdom—seems antithetical to current trends. This is one of the main strategies of the ego—to stay too busy to listen to the Self. The ego drowns out the inner voice of truth with conditioned habits of obsession, busymindness, and distraction. Through the thought system, the ego maintains its equilibrium by negating anything that disagrees with its beliefs and habits.

In order to be your true Self you must get to know your Self. In order to know your Self you must take time to reflect and listen within. When your mind is still, you are in the zone and thus able to perform at higher levels, with the tremendous benefit of Universal Intelligence. Your life becomes more creative, inspired, and purposeful when you live from your true Self and the insight and wisdom that comes with it. Without reflection, you

are like the conditioned people of Huxley's *Brave New World*.
Reflection is the tool to sustain your connection to the true Self
and avoid falling back into the hypnotic effects of the collective
unconsciousness and your own ego.

Trust Your Insights, Inspiration, and Wisdom

Without trust, your insights will never mature into inspired action.
Trust is faith in action, faith in your true Self. When you trust
your wisdom, you operate from the knowing and certainty necessary to turn your ideas into realities.

When Mahatma Gandhi had the insight that India could liberate itself from British rule by producing its own salt, this simple idea sparked the spirit of change throughout India. In an act
of civil disobedience, thousands marched 248 miles to the sea in
the Dandi Salt March, which called for a refusal to pay the salt
tax—a symbolic gesture to assert India's independence. By refus-
ing to resort to violence they were able to break the control of
the British, who eventually turned over power to the Indian government in 1947.

Gandhi *trusted* his inspiration. He began his march after fast-
ing a very long period and could barely walk. At first only his
loyal followers joined him. By the time he arrived in Bombay
and the Indian Ocean, there were thousands joined in courage
and resolve to resist British rule. Thus began the independence
of a nation. Gandhi didn't know if anyone would follow him to
the sea; he just did what he felt inspired to do in the moment.

When you are operating from the truth of insight and wisdom, you don't know specifically what the outcome will be. You
simply trust that it is the right thing to do and know that it is
what you must do. This is what resolve is—deciding to move in
a direction without knowledge of the specific form it will take.
If you continue to do what is right in your heart, your life will
eventually manifest the truth of your insights.

Transform Spirit into Form through the
Courage to Act from the True Self

Millions of people throughout time have had inspired thoughts and insights from the true Self that never became a reality because they lacked the courage to act on their thoughts. Instead, they lived lives of regret and unfulfilled dreams.

What does it mean to have the courage to act from the true Self? Courage is a natural outcome of seeing the truth of what needs to be done and doing it. It's that simple. As I mentioned earlier, many times a person we think of as courageous has had no thought of courage; to them it's common sense. We make too much of courage and turn people into superheroes. Thus we diminish ourselves and our innate capacity to perform the same courageous acts as any well-known hero or famous person.

Living fearlessly can be something as ordinary as having the courage to say "No" to an invitation to dinner or an event when your inner wisdom says "No" and your habit of obligation says, "Yes I really can't let them down." Or, having the courage to go against the group when your instinct tells you they are wrong.

Beware of the Ego Taking Credit (Symptoms:
Pride, Superiority, Judgment, Control)

I know of and know personally many people who, by acting from their true Selves, became successful and famous as authors, seminar leaders, business entrepreneurs, entertainers, and athletes. However, what began with a passion for creating or following an idea turned into an ego trip. They may still have remained successful, but their success was diminished by pride, arrogance, superiority, greed for more, and sometimes doing what sounded like the right thing as a way to feed the ego. The ego is insatiable. If we operate from it, no amount of money, power, or recognition is enough, and thus we sow the seeds of our downfall.

Getting everything you desire is much like what happens in the Greek myth of King Midas, who loved gold so much he made a wish that everything he touched would turn to gold. At first he was happy and proud of his accomplishment when he turned a twig into gold. He was so delighted he held a large banquet for his kingdom, but every time he tried to eat anything it turned to gold. He begged the gods to remove his wish, which became his curse when he turned his most beloved daughter into gold.

When you act from your true Self, you too become lucky and your dreams begin to manifest as reality. Heed the example of King Midas, and don't let your pride spoil your joy. Humility is the antidote to pride. Keep perspective by remembering that your success is the result not of ego, but of getting the ego out of the way so the Self can do its natural work.

Be Willing to Act from Your True Self, Even When Others Don't Understand or Approve

Acting from the true Self is no popularity contest. More often than not, when you act from true insight you will challenge the status quo. As a result, when you speak the truth the ego is often offended, angry, and punishing.

Recently I was with a mother and her daughter. The mom had just had a fight with her husband and was trying to justify her anger to her six-year-old daughter. After a long series of rationalizations, the wise six-year-old said, "Mommy, listen to Daddy's heart and you will know he loves you and then you won't be mad anymore." The mom was stunned at the power of her daughter's words but quickly dismissed them in her mind as a child not understanding the complexity of human relationships.

The next day when she realized the wisdom of her daughter's words, I said to her, "Out of the mouths of babes. . . . " She now uses this as a great story about her own realization of how her ego gets triggered. Young children, old wise people, and the powerless are often the greatest spokespersons for truth, but they are seldom listened to and often are chastised for telling the truth.

When you identify with your true inner Spirit, you know that nothing can hurt or threaten you. When you don't feel threatened by the thought of losing others' approval or losing security (financial or physical), and you are certain of your insights, courage is a natural outcome. If I don't have my ego on the line (my false sense of self based on what others think of me and what I think I have), I have nothing to lose. In the lyrics of Kris Kristofferson, "Freedom's just another word for nothing left to lose." We can only lose what is not us, we can't lose our true Self—it is beyond this world of form.

Forgive Yourself When You Slip Back into Ego Habits

Everyone moves in and out of awareness of when they are caught up in habitual patterns of ego thinking. Even if you have made a commitment to living from your true Self and living a fearless life, you will have moments when you are not living true to your Self. The reason for these slips is to *transform belief into knowing*, and the only way you can turn a belief into a knowing is to go through an experience. Therefore, what appear to be mistakes are really ways to raise your awareness of your habits and highlight the difference between living from the ego and living from the true Self.

Each time I fall back into a reaction from my ego, it feels worse and worse. If this happens to you, don't worry; it's supposed to feel that way! That is because the more you live from your true Self, the more living in the ego feels like the awful, painful, and unnatural illusion it is. This is a good thing, because you now know what it feels like to be your true Self, and the contrast between the two states is very evident.

It used to feel normal to live from your ego—to be afraid, to worry, to be stressed, to feel powerless, to be angry. Now it begins to feel toxic, and you recognize it as that—this is a sign of health, not of slipping back. Falling back into old habits is really just a process of discovery and cleansing. It takes multiple cycles in the washing machine to separate the dirt from the clothes. The same is true with discovery of the true Self. Each time you fall into old habits, your awareness becomes more acute, more refined as to what is true and what is false.

When you understand this, forgiving yourself will be a piece of cake. You will get over the old habit more quickly, feel less pain about it, and move on with your life, from the stance of the true Self. And then you will fall again, and again. Each time it will get easier and faster to get up and forgive yourself. If you don't forgive yourself for being a human being with an ego, you won't be able to forgive others.

Forgive Others for Their Ego-Based Actions by Seeing Their Innocence and the Illusion of Separate Realities

Once you are able to forgive yourself, you will be far more able to forgive others. Another way of saying this is that once you love yourself enough to see your own innocence, to see that you are in the process of discovering what it means to be your Self, the easier it will be to see that everyone else is in the same place. Everyone is a Divine Being who either doesn't yet know or is in the process of uncovering the truth of who they are inside— Spirit in human form.

When you are able to see how easy it is to become hypnotized by your own conditioned thought system and the ego, it is far easier to see that everyone else is doing the same thing. The more afraid people are, the more likely they will be to get caught up in the habits of ego—blaming, judging, striking out in anger or violence, feeling powerless, or giving up. When you recognize this from your true Self, you feel compassion and forgiveness. This protects you from other people's ignorance and lack of awareness. It allows you to be in the world of many scared people, but not be adversely affected by them. Compassion is love in the face of suffering. If someone is in their ego, no matter how deluded they are, they are suffering.

Take Responsibility for Whatever You Create

Last, take responsibility for whatever you create, whether it is from your true Self *or* from your ego. Taking responsibility doesn't mean you feel guilty if you created from the ego or that you feel pride if you created from the true Self. It just means that you are responsible for whatever you do in life. Don't blame it on your ego, or the devil, or your parents' way of raising you, or that you were off that day. Whatever you do in life is your creation. If you don't take responsibility for what you have created, you will be fated to continue recreating it unconsciously.

When you create from the ego unknowingly and then realize it and take responsibility for it, you turn the experience into a deeper insight. This is how you turn living from the ego into living from the true Self. If you don't take responsibility, you will have to blame someone or something else, and then you rob yourself of a greater awareness and discovery of the true Self. Unfortunately, if you don't take responsibility for your mistakes, you continue to repeat them. The act of responsibility is an act of awareness and a choice to let go of the habit.

Final Comments

Ultimately, we are all here on Earth to discover and express the essence of our Being. Through fear and our addiction to it, we lose our awareness of our true Selves and become prisoners of our ego-based thought systems. Now is the time for all of us to become free of the fear that has kept us from joy, from creativity, from peace, from the courage to be honest. It is time to do the inspired thing, which is to live our life's purpose.

I hope this book and the ideas, principles, and guidelines it offers will allow you to begin the journey of discovery and ultimately the living of a fearless life. I leave you with these final words:

Come out of your prison of fear.
No longer be shackled to addiction.
Know your Self, be your Self, trust your Self.
Courageously be your fullest expression of who you are in the world.
Let your brilliance shine into the world and inspire all who witness you to do the same.
There is only one you in the world—be your Self.

About the Author

Joseph Bailey, M.A., L.P., is the author of several books, including *The Serenity Principle, The Speed Trap, Slowing Down to the Speed of Life* (with Richard Carlson), and *Slowing Down to the Speed of Love.* For the past thirty-five years he has worked as a psychotherapist, seminar leader, and consultant to a variety of healthcare, business, education, and government agencies in the area of mental well-being. He has been an adjunct instructor at the University of Minnesota and St. Mary's University. His writing and his consulting all focus on helping people see their innate capacity for balance, wisdom, and happiness. He lives in St. Paul, MN. Visit Bailey at *www.joebaileyandassociates.com.*

To Our Readers

Conari Press, an imprint of Red Wheel/Weiser, publishes books on topics ranging from spirituality, personal growth, and relationships to women's issues, parenting, and social issues. Our mission is to publish quality books that will make a difference in people's lives—how we feel about ourselves and how we relate to one another. We value integrity, compassion, and receptivity, both in the books we publish and in the way we do business.

Our readers are our most important resource, and we value your input, suggestions, and ideas about what you would like to see published. Please feel free to contact us, to request our latest book catalog, or to be added to our mailing list.

Conari Press
An imprint of Red Wheel/Weiser, LLC
500 Third Street, Suite 230
San Francisco, CA 94107
www.redwheelweiser.com